What others are saying about BELIEF THE...

"In this remarkable book, DeGoede and D.... how beliefs originate in childhood, how they gradually empower or disempower people's lives, and how they can be changed. These are not new ideas, but the authors inclusion of spiritual and environmental issues make **Belief Therapy** one of the most practical and timely self-help books available today."

Stanley Krippner, Ph.D.
Professor of Psychology Saybrook Institute
Co-author, The Mythic Path
Author and co-author of over 700 publications
Who's who in America
Who's who in the World
Internationally known Researcher and Psychologist

"**Dr. DeGoede's book spells out the obvious. In fact, like higher order math, it is so simple and so obvious that almost no one can see it.** He describes how our lives are dic -tated by conflicting beliefs (organizing principles) that largely go unnoticed. Rather than use beliefs, we are used by them. He shows how to choose the organizing principles that serve our highest aspirations and let the others go. **In short, he explains how to escape belief jail and create the life experiences we truly want.**"

Gary Emery, Ph.D.
Owner and Director of Los Angeles Center For Cognitive Therapy
Co-author with Aaron Beck of Anxiety Disorders and Phobias: A
Cognitive Perspective
Over 66 publications, audio and video tapes

"**In their wonderful and timely new book, Belief Therapy,** DeGoede and Drews show with remarkable clarity not only that we really do create our own reality, but that we can learn to supplant our learned destructive ideas and beliefs with new positive and healing images, both of ourselves and of the world around us. I especially liked the thoughts expressed in the chapter on Religion and Spirituality that we should stop blaming God or a non-existent Satan for our problems and learn to accept responsibility for our perceptions and for our own actions."

Ellwood W. Norquist
Author of We Are One: A Challenge to Traditional Christianity

"DeGoede and Drews' theory clearly illustrates the impact our beliefs hold over our lives and futures. Dealing with trauma or 'abuse moments', is a crucial concept in healing intrapsychic pain. __Belief Therapy__ gives one the needed infor - mation which leads us on the road to recovery."

Jennifer L. Firestone, Ph.D.
Clinical Psychology
Specialist in women's issues and trauma
Stephenville, Texas

"DeGoede and Drews do a very thorough job of examining the significant role which self-awareness plays in all our lives. __Belief Therapy__ clearly communicates that the inability to over - come the limitations of your belief system is the biggest obstacle to achieving true happiness."

Mitchell J. Cohen, M.F.C.C.
Marriage, Family and Child Counselor

"Bravo DeGoede for steering clear of technical jargon, and putting together an __astute__, comprehensive, and motivational book with the potential to enhance and save lives. Long awaited; something fresh and loaded with personality."

Michael Gantenbien, N.C.A.C.II, C.A.D.C., I.C.A.D.C.
National Certified Drug And Alcohol Counselor

"I am more than pleased to see that in their **Belief Therapy** *(love that title!)* ***DeGoede and Drews present in a very clear, emotional yet perceptive and creative ways elemental insights into what it means to be human.*** *They show us how to become more freely and consciously awake as we understand that each one of us does indeed create our own reality. With that precious knowledge we can set ourselves free to better become the innately creative, illimitable creatures that we are gifted at birth to be. A most challenging endeavor indeed to get to know ourselves!"*

Robert F. Butts
Co-Creator of the Seth/Jane Roberts books

"Dr. DeGoede's book, **Belief Therapy,** *reflects his humanistic approach which gives new meaning to personal empowerment and possibilities. Dr. DeGoede has the ability to simplify complex issues allowing for exploration of existing beliefs.* ***Using the approach as discussed in his book, may precipitate con - crete changes and bring renewed direction to life."***

Karen Wardell, M.Ed., B.S.N.
Consultant to California State Department of Education
Administrative Program Specialist, Special Education

"I believe a great addition to every prescription written by a physician should include a copy of <u>Belief Therapy</u>, *by Daniel L. DeGoede.* As a Registered Nurse, I was especially interested in reading his section on 'Health.' While reading Dr. DeGoede's ideas on how one's body responds to one's beliefs, I kept thinking, 'Wow, this is very simple, and most of all, it makes sense!' Everyone needs to take responsibility for his or her own physical health, including health professionals. As we learn more about the physical diseases that effect us, we cannot overlook the role our psyche plays in regaining and maintaining health. **Good stuff for every patient in sickness and health!"**

Robert B. Renno, RN
Director of Clinical Services
Charter Behavioral Health Systems

"Dr. DeGoede's explanations of the growing violence commit - ted by children in this country are not only accurate but also frightening when one understands the lack of emotion, conscience and empathy they feel for their victims. **When parents truly realize what their children are doing, and why, the only solution to eliminating exhibited violence and all acting-out behaviors is to learn, implement, and believe in Dr. DeGoede's techniques on 'parenting.'** If more parents prac - ticed these methods, the need for more programs such as those run by my company for at-risk children would dramatically decline. All of our country's children would be better."

Amy S. Harrison
Vice Chairman, President of Children's Comprehensive Services, Inc.
A publicly traded $110,000,000 company designs and operates
programs for The "At Risk" youth in 12 states.

"Dr. DeGoede's book offers clear and comprehensive descriptions of the various beliefs we adopt as a child which can either hinder or empower us. As a result of his research and fascinating case studies, we can begin to recognize and understand how we can identify positive things we can do to help ourselves."

Karen L. Hoag, Ed.D. (a.b.d.)
Administrator, San Bernardino City Schools

"We like to think that we make our ideas and make our beliefs but in truth our ideas and our **beliefs are what make us. Dr. DeGoede's book clarifies** this point in a highly readable, com - prehensible, and most of all, simple fashion. **It is a must!"**

Patrick MacAfee, Ph.D.
Marriage, Child and Family Counselor
Certified Addictions Specialist
American Academy of Health Care Providers

"Belief Therapy *is a book that should be in every college and high school library!* DeGoede and Drews have created an excellent, dynamic tool for personal empowerment. A book about courage and hope, written from personal philosophy and experience, it is a belief system about beliefs. Shining through the pages and chapters is a concept of healing the 'division and separation; from ourselves, from each other and from all life.' **This is a valuable and useful work and will have deep impact on readers."**

Jane Van Roekel, R.S.P.
Religious Science Practitioner
High School Counselor, Metaphysics Teacher
Spiritual counselor and Practitioner

"Dr. DeGoede's book Belief Therapy brings to mind the old adage you are what you think.' *This is a significant factor with addictions and codependency. This book offers techniques and insights to change our beliefs about ourselves which is an essential element associated with 12 Step Programs."*

Jan Fagerquist, MS, C.A.S
Chemical Dependency Program Coordinator

"Belief Therapy *is based on concepts which the lay person will easily understand.* Dr. DeGoede presents practical ways of addressing difficult problems and his methods can be utilized after the first few pages of reading. **This is a significant book which gives people tools to utilize outside of the therapy session."**

Jama Ellen Briscoe, Ph.D.
Clinical Psychologist

"Simple and Elegant. *A powerful look at how we develop dysfunctional beliefs and, more importantly, how we can loosen their grip over our lives.* **This book shows a pathway to enhance pleasure and restore meaning to our lives** *by revealing childhood misconceptions, limiting beliefs, self-defeating behaviors and replacing them with empowering images, constructive thoughts, and productive actions.* **A wise and practical text from a seasoned psychotherapist."**

Craig Lambdin, MA, M.F.C.C.
Executive Director of My Family Incorporated Recovery Center
Multi Program Chemical Dependency Treatment Center

"DeGoede and Drews' book **Belief Therapy**, illustrates in the most simplistic of terms the dysfunctional dance that goes on between codependents and dependents, as well as the core beliefs in both partners which precipitate the behavior. Bravo! DeGoede and Drews **Belief Therapy** *not only helps the reader to iden - tify destructive core beliefs, but also enlightens and chal - lenges the reader to make positive changes in their core belief systems.*"

Vickie Wilson, C.A.C.
Certification: Alcohol and Drug Studies
Family Counselor

"*I found* **Belief Therapy** *to be a very easy read.* I especial - ly liked the conversational style of the piece. DeGoede gives solid practical advice toward managing behaviors. I like that. **Belief Therapy** *further enables the reader to get something real from the information. I truly enjoyed the chapter on parenting. I believe good parenting and good classroom teaching are one in the same. **Cool book for people to carry around like a handbook.**"

Laurel MacTaggart, BA
3rd Grade Teacher

"Liberating oneself to be able to freely act upon one's world is the theme of Dr. DeGoede's book. This book gives you the insight to start this journey. **Dr. DeGoede offers a guide to a rich life in simplistic form and is able to make his teachings under - stood by all segments of society.**"

Edward F. Reed, Ed.D.
Director of After Care Recovery Center

"**Dr. DeGoede's book is excellent. He converts the most complicated situations into easy to read, understandable reality terms. This book is a page turner, once you begin you cannot stop.**"

Jeff McDonald, C.A.D.A.C., C.E.A.P.
Certified Alcohol and Drug Counselor
Certified Employee Assistance Program

"As the Clinical Director of an Adolescent and Children's Program, **Belief Therapy** really hits the mark with the chapter on 'Parenting.' This will not only be mandatory reading for all our therapists, but for all parents we work with.** The most influential characteristic we possess, whether as a therapist, parent, or person involved with children and adolescents is what we **Believe."**

Jesse R. Mellor, MA, C.A.S.
Clinical Director / Child & Adolescent Services
Veteran Memorial Medical Center Connecticut

"Violence in America, from Dr. DeGoede's book **Belief Therapy, was very exciting to read. This book cuts right to the center core of what society is battling with, it just makes sense that everyone has a certain degree of control in their lives."**

Joe Morales
13 Years Law Enforcement, LA County Sheriffs Dept.

"Belief Therapy clearly spells out people's role in their own upset.** More importantly, it also points out people's role in their own recovery of happiness and meaning in life. **This book can be an asset for people in their self-help library.** Thanks for the opportunity to read this interesting book."

Gordon F. West, Ph.D., Ed.S.
Eisenhower Medical Center, Dept. of Pastoral Care
Chaplain and Employee Assistance Coordinator
Adjunct Instructor, College of the Desert, Palm Desert, California

"Dr. DeGoede's book, **Belief Therapy, shows his keen understanding of the emotional process and the power of the human mind to be instrumental in self healing.** Dr. DeGoede's experiences and observations provide an informed and relevant perspective. Overall, his book provides an opportunity for better understanding the complexities of the developmental process and gives practical guidance to implement improvement."

Gary Osantowski, L.C.S.W.
Licensed Clinical Social Worker

"DeGoede and Drews' new book describes in clear and readable language the power that belief systems have to shape our lives, and they show us practical psycho-spiritual ways to transform negative beliefs into constructive paths."

Ilene A. Serlin, Ph.D.
Professor of Psychology
National Women's Hall of Fame
Who's Who in Executive & Professional Women
International Who's Who in Medicine
Over 25 Publications/Articles

Personal Testimony

"Enlightening, innovative! Belief Therapy is an invalu - able resource for enhancing the quality of daily living. *A valuable tool to learn the steps to take for making positive changes.* An innovative process that could save your life as it did mine. *Thank you Dr. DeGoede for the profound positive changes this information has made in my life.* For the first time I found happiness because of implementing the resources provided in your book."

Cheryl Aguilar, A.D.N., RN
Critical Care Registered Nurse
Loma Linda University Medical Center

"Never have I read anything on the subject of therapy so clearly and simply and effectively written. *For the first time I understood the definition of codependency and thus my rela - tionship with my son. Simple or not, it evoked in me terrible dreams for three nights. I carefully wrote them down and ana - lyzed them (as I know what treasures these dragons protect) and so gained a thorough understanding of how incest had set me up for being codependent. Through* **Belief Therapy** *I have become free of half a century of anguish and self blame.*"

Betty Paramore
Centerfold, Playboy Magazine
November, 1956

*"**Dr. DeGoede and Danaë are the reason my son is still alive.** This is no book-blurb hyperbole. We came to them as do many parents, with our very broken, multiple-drug dependent child. They showed us, first-hand, the life saving potential of* <u>**Belief Therapy**</u>. **This book, like their program, is a miracle. It elucidates in clear, simple concepts the profound truths that led my son to a life of clarity.** *It's not panacea, but it is the most effective system to date in the treatment of substance abuse. I say this not as an academic, but as a soldier on the front-line. I saw my son through all the steps and substances and inpa - tient miasma that now comprises this nation's approach to drug abuse. I have living testimony of my son, when so many of his friends have fallen along the way.* **Their program is the only one that works. The only one."**

Melody Tanner-Clark, MA

Author of Tomorrow, There Will Be Everything: Nanotechnology and the Future, popular, pub date TBA
Life among the Red-Colored Drapes, novel, Clarion Press pending
A Room in the House of the Ancestors, novel, Clarion Press 1995
Rose of Ashes, novel. Clarion Press. 1993
The Dark Shadows Companion, entertainment reference, Pomegranate Press, Ltd., 1990
Guide to the Green Hornet, entertainment reference, Champion Press, 1991

BELIEF THERAPY
A Guide to
Enhancing
Everyday
Life

Daniel L. DeGoede, Ph.D.
with Danaë Drews, C.A.S.

E.D.L.
Productions

An *original* publication of

Post Office Box 786
Lake Elsinore, CA 92531

Library of Congress Catalog Card Number: 98-92615

ISBN: 0-9663745-0-9

Disclaimer
Belief Therapy, "A Guide To Enhancing Everyday Life",
is educational in nature. It is designed to offer the
reader the opportunity to explore their own beliefs. It
is not designed to substitute for needed medical,
psychiatric, or psychological treatment.

First Printing 1998
10 9 8 7 6 5 4 3

Acknowledgements

I first want to thank my <u>entire</u> family for their continuing emotional support and encouragement. Second, my wife Judy, for being who she is; third, my daughter and co-author Danaë for her expertise and undying enthusiasm; next my son Damian for his wonderful poems; and finally, I dedicate this book to my father who was unable to be here for its publication. Thank you all! I love you!

A PIECE OF LIFE

A single rose before my eyes
It bleeds of red beneath blue skies
Just a flower it may seem
Yet helps to find a once lost dream
Petals frosted with morning dew
Last living rose pulled just for you

ALL POETRY WRITTEN BY

Award Winning Poet

Damian K. DeGoede

Editors Choice Award 1996
Editors Choice Award 1998

CONTENTS

PREFACE

For approximately the last 30 years of my life I have been involved in the "business" of psychology. I have throughout this time been student, teacher, and "helper". In these roles I have devoted much of my life to understanding and utilizing various methods and philosophies of psychology to help people learn to change their lives in useful and positive ways. Through these years of study and practice, I have begun to recognize certain common principles of life that must be understood and utilized to take control of our lives and improve our day to day reality.

My task has been to organize these underlying truths in a way that allows them to be understood and utilized to improve everyday life. If I have been able to accomplish that task in any measurable way, then I have succeeded and owe a great debt to the many and diverse students of human nature who have preceded me.

INTRODUCTION

WHAT IS BELIEF THERAPY?

Belief therapy is based on the idea that our beliefs create our reality. This means that deeply held ideas and beliefs about life, that are often unconscious and unexamined, affect our daily emotions, thoughts, and behaviors. The importance of this concept is that it allows people to once again feel in control of their lives. If my beliefs are creating my everyday reality, and I am able to discover, examine, and change these beliefs, then I am in charge of my life to a much greater degree than previously thought.

WHERE DO THESE BELIEFS COME FROM?

It is common knowledge that our early childhood experiences have a powerful effect on our lives. What is not so easy to understand is why this is so. The reason we are so influenced by our early experiences is because that is where our first beliefs developed. It is just these beliefs that are likely to be unconscious, unexamined, and irrational. As children we accept these beliefs as *truths* and then feel and act accordingly. If our childhood beliefs or ideas are not examined, they become a basis for our adult experience. This experience then seems to confirm the limiting beliefs we hold about ourselves, reinforcing them in our everyday life. How many of us are still responding to childhood comments such as; "Big boys don't cry", "Be a good girl", "Don't be afraid", "Quit acting stupid", or "You'll never amount to anything"? How many of our daily decisions regarding parenting, health, relationships, finances, and life in general are influenced by these, often irrational ideas about ourselves?

As children we were influenced by the beliefs of parents, teachers, religious leaders, peers, and the mass media. These ideas were accepted as *truths* at a time when we were too young and unaware to evaluate them properly. They have consequently acted as powerful hypnotic suggestions, influencing our daily actions, thoughts, and emotions. Worse, as we believe these ideas to be truths and not simply ideas about reality, we never examine or consider the possibility that they can be changed, thereby changing our daily life experience. This dooms us to live out a "fate" created by others, at a time in our life when we could not evaluate or defend ourselves from this influence.

It is only by becoming aware of our conscious and unconscious beliefs that we can gain the ability to be free from these limiting ideas and create our lives, as we choose, in the present. Freud said, "the unconscious must become conscious." In this he was right, we cannot change that of which we are unaware. Choice and freedom come through awareness. Without awareness we are destined to repeat the same self-defeating behaviors and to experience the negative emotions created by forgotten, irrational beliefs.

Limiting beliefs affect every area of our lives. The first step towards change is awareness and recognition of these destructive ideas. Now let's examine the areas of our life affected and consider what we can do about it.

1

THE SELF

Please take some time out of your life
Spend it pure, alone for once
No one there to put you down or say you're wrong
Yet no one there to pick you up and say you're right
Just one chance, just one time to be yourself
so with this soul that you keep locked in your body
this time let it free, break the lock and let it go and
use the power that you hold

*T*he most private and personal place to begin is with our ideas and feelings about ourselves. How we think about ourselves determines how we feel about ourselves. How we feel about ourselves determines how we feel moment to moment, day to day, and year to year.

If I have been taught to believe I am stupid, this belief will determine how I feel and behave in virtually every area of my life. I will not try for promotions. I will not speak up in a crowd. I either will not go to college or I will predictably fail if I do. New ideas will scare me because I will be afraid I won't understand them. New people and experiences will scare me as I will fear judgment or failure.

If I believe I am ugly, too fat, or too thin, I will feel self conscious. I will believe other people are talking about me even when they are not and because of my belief in my unattractiveness, I will carry my body and present myself to others in unflattering ways. I will feel inadequate in dating and relationship settings. I will judge and hate myself and constantly be trying to change even while I feel hopeless, helpless, and unable to change.

Beliefs that I am weak or sickly will create obsessions with my health and I will worry about every sniffle, ache, or pain. I will limit my activities and enjoyment of life and stifle those around me with a chronic over-concern with sickness. Constant daily obsessive thoughts will become unconscious reminders to my body that I am *not* healthy. Eventually, I will produce the very symptoms that I fear by my preoccupation and obsession.

If early conditioning created the beliefs that I am too angry, tearful, loud, or even too quiet, I will lose

7

confidence in my natural emotions. This will cause me to distrust myself and to believe I am inferior to others because of my feelings. I will then attempt to suppress or deny these "bad" feelings until I am forced to act them out in some inappropriate flight into rage, violence, or depression. As I grow older, I will learn more "sophisticated" ways of blocking my emotions such as alcohol, drugs, or other compulsive behaviors.

Negative comments about physical appearance and ability create limiting beliefs leading to poor self-and body-image. When children are teased for being too fat, ugly, skinny, clumsy, tall, freckle-faced, or bow-legged, they develop problems in self perception. Negative statements about physical health such as; "Why are you always sick?", "You're too weak", and "What's wrong with you now?" create obsessions with health, and lack of pleasure in life.

In the case of childhood illnesses where children are often taught to believe they are "special" because of their illness, comments like; "You almost died", "You're not like other children", or "We sacrificed everything for you", cause children to begin to feel different, which creates feelings of isolation and aloneness. Beliefs of being "sickly" cause over dependence on parents, hospitals, and doctors, preventing these children from feeling self-sufficient, capable, and independent. Then, when the parents of children with health problems overprotect them, this increases their belief in their inadequacy and dependency on others.

Critical statements about intellectual abilities, such as; "You're lazy", "You're stupid", or "Why aren't you smart like your brother?" create life long doubts about our ability to perform in school, at work, socially, and individually. We learn to see ourselves as inadequate and inferior in a society that above all stresses intellectual achievement.

Disapproving remarks about creative accomplishments like; "Don't waste your time with that stuff", "You'll need a real job to support a family", "You can't carry a tune", or "You're too slow to play sports", block our natural talents. This causes us to doubt ourselves and limit our real achievements in art, music, and sports.

Criticism regarding sexuality and sexual body parts often lead to powerful feelings of shame and guilt. Parents who are uncomfortable with their own sexuality and eliminative body parts will influence their children, through attitudes, comments and behaviors, to think like them. The negative effect on children (and later adults) from these judgmental ideas has both long-and short-term damaging results on our body image and general self-esteem. Comments such as; "Don't touch yourself there", "You'll go to hell", "You're bad"... "dirty"... "nasty", lead to self-judgment, confusion, and shame. When these natural feelings, thoughts, and behaviors are so harshly judged it creates long lasting problems that negatively affect our lives.

The negative ideas and beliefs *most* damaging to the overall person are the ones affecting our emotions. Children are often taught to distrust their feelings before they are able to walk. What is more personal, intimate, and closely identified with the self than our emotions? When parents model suppression and distrust of their emotions, children are taught the same. When children hear; "Shut up", "Be still", "Don't be a cry baby", "Don't laugh", or "Don't scream", they learn to distrust themselves. This is usual in our society, even the leaders of our country are admired and rewarded for their ability to keep a straight face, maintain their composure, and to be "cool under fire."

When we are unsuccessful at blocking our emotions through the defenses of denial, repression, compulsive work, gambling, sex, drugs, or alcohol, we go to *The Doctor.* This usually leads to a prescription drug scientifically designed to make us more calm, less depressed, more tired, or happier. In other words, a drug designed to more effectively block our natural feelings, which then continues the pervasive and destructive pattern of self-betrayal.

We have even been taught to distrust our body's natural impulses, desires, and needs. Our bodies naturally know how much to eat, when to sleep, when to go to the bathroom, and when to exercise. There is a wisdom of the body that we have learned to ignore which causes serious problems in health, diet, and addictions. This pervasive distrust of our body has created an over-reliance on others such as doctors, teachers, and scientists. This lack of personal responsibility ultimately leads to decreased health, both physically and psychologically.

Early directions that taught us to mistrust our natural appetites, desires, impulses, and sensations were often in the form of commands: "Clean up your plate", "You eat too much", "Can't you hold it?", "You need more rest", or "You sleep too much." Parents who did not trust themselves further modeled these limiting ideas with constant obsessive compulsive behaviors. Mother may have always been on a diet and chronically exercising, while father slept all day and ate everything in sight. These directions and behaviors encouraged a deep distrust in our natural feelings leading to the betrayal of the self.

Did you find yourself agreeing with any of these above limiting beliefs and remembering how you learned these destructive ideas? Now imagine a life where you wake up every morning feeling trust and acceptance in yourself. How different life would be! Now that you understand that you were systematically taught to distrust and dislike yourself, let's find out how to reverse that process.

THE BEGINNING

There are many ways to change these limiting and destructive ideas from our past. First, it is necessary to know which beliefs need to be changed. All of our old ideas and beliefs are not bad. Many of them have been very useful to us and have reliably allowed us to be successful in various parts of our life. Examples of useful beliefs are beliefs that help us to feel better about ourselves and to perform better in life, such as; "I'm real smart", "I deserve to succeed", "I'm okay just the way I am", and "It's okay to feel like that." Our positive beliefs have encouraged us to do well and have allowed us to feel good about ourselves. One way to know which beliefs we want to keep and which we need to change is to make lists of all our beliefs in different areas of our lives. Since we are now examining feelings about the self, this would be a good time to start listing all the different ways you think and feel about *yourself*. While many of your deeply held beliefs and ideas about yourself will not be immediately apparent to you, a closer look at your conscious, everyday thoughts and feelings will help show you where to look.

For example, if you find yourself avoiding new tasks or promotions at work by telling yourself; "I can't do this", you most likely have core beliefs of inadequacy and failure. These beliefs probably come from early childhood experiences of being told, "You're stupid", "What's wrong with you?", or "Can't you do anything right?" or, conversely you may have learned to believe that you were inadequate by being over protected and having everything done for you. Parents who over criticize or over protect their children undermine the child's emerging self identity. By examining your daily, conscious ideas, thoughts, behaviors, and feelings, you will begin to see the limiting beliefs that continue to reinforce these old feelings of inadequacy. By seeing these limiting ideas you are taking the first step towards changing them to more fulfilling and life enhancing ones.

There are many ways that old beliefs influence our lives. Another example would be a couple who are in a committed and loving relationship, have been happily married for several years, but continue to feel awkward, embarrassed, or just "not right" when it comes to giving and receiving sexual pleasure. They know intellectually that there is nothing "wrong" with what they are doing, but emotionally they are unable to relax and enjoy themselves, or their partner, in a sexual way. These problems usually stem from early childhood beliefs about sex being bad, dirty, sinful, or wrong. Although, they may "know" that now that they are married sex is supposed to be okay, it doesn't feel like it. This is because they continue to respond emotionally and behaviorally to these incorrect and outdated ideas about sexuality that they learned as children. Without examining and consciously disregarding these limiting childhood ideas, problems of this kind are not likely to end.

Now that you have begun to look closely at your daily thoughts, behaviors, and emotions, and have written down lists of both beliefs you want to change and beliefs you want to keep, it is time to begin the process of change that will lead you towards a more rewarding and fulfilling life.

SELF-HYPNOSIS

One powerful and useful way to begin to change your beliefs is through the technique of hypnosis. First, let's consider what hypnosis is. Hypnosis is the art of influencing a person's actions, ideas, or emotions, typically while they are in a highly focused, often vulnerable or suggestible state wherein they cannot easily, consciously defend themselves from the influence. It's a little like brainwashing and it's precisely what happened to us as children. We were in a highly vulnerable and suggestible state called childhood and were at the mercy of other's repeated commands, suggestions, and ideas about reality. This caused us to form our views about reality without being able or capable of deciding for ourselves whether those views were accurate or not. We automatically accepted the accurate with the inaccurate, the rational with the irrational, the useful with the destructive. But, if these "hypnotic techniques" worked so well to influence us in a negative way, why can't they be used now, consciously, to influence us positively? They can, and self-hypnosis and visual imagery are powerful techniques for changing limiting beliefs and reinforcing useful beliefs. How do we use these techniques in a useful way to de-program ourselves and help change the limiting beliefs that are negatively affecting our lives?

To utilize self-hypnosis and visual imagery, take ten to fifteen minutes per day and practice visualizing and imagining the changes you wish to make. Begin with an area of your life in which you are experiencing difficulty, such as physical appearance or poor body image. List all of the beliefs that you are aware of that have to do with how you feel about your body, both the negative and the positive. Go over those beliefs consciously and select from them the ones that you wish to challenge.

For example, a man that is taught to feel unattractive because he is short, can learn to stand more erect, carry himself as if he were taller, and learn to feel taller. He can imagine himself walking tall and self-confident. By doing so he will feel better about himself and others will react accordingly. He cannot, through these techniques, make himself grow extra inches after he has reached maturity, but he can learn to carry himself in a way that causes others to respond as if he had those extra inches. He can also learn to appreciate and accept himself so those "extra inches" are no longer necessary for his self-esteem.

When a woman has been taught since she was a small child that her only value in life is her ability to look a particular way, her self-identity, self-worth, and body image are all connected with her appearance. Of course, the way she thinks she needs to look is the stereotype of the society in which she lives. In this society, she needs to look like a 21-year-old model represented on the cover of all the current magazines at the newsstand. In order to change this limiting belief, it is first useful to ask an appropriate question: "Is this accurate?" Does she need to look this way to be accepted and loved? Or is that simply something she learned? By consciously challenging this limiting belief, she is then able to consider other ways of thinking. After realizing that self-esteem, acceptance, and love are not necessarily connected with body image and appearance, it is possible to then evaluate the accuracy of her body image.

To evaluate her body image, she can list all of the areas of her physical appearance about which she feels good. She can daily visualize these attractive parts of her body and imagine that others notice them also. Next, she can list the parts of her physical appearance that she has decided she wants to change. For example, if she determines that she is overweight and she has been told that she is fat and unattractive, she can use self-hypnosis as a vehicle to change her body appearance. Then she can list the areas of her life that she feels good about other than her physical appearance and by doing so recognize that she has value separate from her outward form. By recognizing and consciously challenging these limiting ideas, she begins to question both the accuracy of her body image and the connection that she has with her body image and her self-esteem.

By spending just ten minutes a day clearly focused, without distractions, and in a relaxed state, concentrate on the changes that you want. Visualize them taking place *right now.* Find a word or phrase that captures the desired change. Repeat this over and over and feel the change beginning *right now.* Remember that you are implanting new, healthy beliefs into your unconscious and that they will be materialized. After the exercise, let it go with the confidence that these new beliefs will create the desired outward effects.

Experiment with different images and/or phrases until they "feel" right. Have confidence in this process and continue it until you are completely satisfied with your outward circumstances.

AWARENESS AND SELF-TALK

Another way to change limiting beliefs and ideas is to consciously pay attention to your daily thought processes. We regularly and unconsciously make negative comments to ourselves based on old core beliefs. If you listen to yourself talk, it will give you an idea of where you need to work to change your limiting beliefs.

You will find that the "critical parent" inside of you responds to critical parents from your past as if they are here now. If your mother or father said, "You're too stupid to do anything right", or "You're never going to succeed",

You'll find yourself saying: "Well, I'm just too stupid to do this", "I'll never amount to anything", or "Everybody does it better than me." These are all self-talk statements that come from limiting beliefs you learned at a young age and then never consciously examined. Just the act of consciously examining limiting beliefs will allow some of them to drop away. When you see these beliefs in the light of new awareness, many will appear silly, outdated, and clearly not accurate. The very awareness of these beliefs will begin to allow you to make the choice to change them.

Another technique is to begin to *think* differently about yourself. When you think differently about yourself, you will begin to *feel* differently about yourself. Instead of saying "I can't do it", you learn to say, "I will do it." When you notice yourself saying, "I'm too stupid", instead say, "That's just an old idea from the past. It's not reality and it's not about me. It's about something I was taught." Then change your behavior to reflect your *new* belief about yourself.

For example, when you walk into a room and you feel like everyone is looking at you, as if there is something wrong with you, remind yourself that this comes from an old feeling of inadequacy, an old belief that there was something about you that other people found unacceptable. Then remind yourself, "That's only a belief, not reality. These are different people, different situations, and I'm not the same person I was then." Now say to yourself, "I know that they're not looking at me. I know that they're not talking about me", and go into that room and act as if those people accept you, enjoy your company, and are looking forward to being around you. By doing this you carry yourself differently, you respond to them differently, and consequently, they respond to you differently. This begins to change limiting beliefs into new and positive beliefs which enhance your self-esteem and self-image.

BIRDS OF A FEATHER

There are many ways to change old beliefs. Consider the group of people that you are around. If you want to think differently, one way is to be with different people with different ideas. We have a natural tendency to place ourselves in an environment with people who think the way we do. If you think that body appearance means everything, you are likely to hang around with people who believe the same and reinforce your old, limiting ideas. If you think that in order to have a good time you have to do drugs or alcohol, then you will tend to spend time with people who think that way. This enhances the limiting belief and increases "cult like" thinking where everybody around you reinforces the same beliefs you are trying to change.

If you're afraid of your emotions and think emotional expression is bad, then you will avoid people who express their feelings openly because they will trigger emotions in you. Instead, you will seek out people who suppress their emotions, reinforcing your idea that the way to live is to hold everything in.

Or if you believe that you are always sick and disease (dis-ease) is thrust upon you and that you will never be healthy, you will spend your time with people who think alike. You will swap symptoms with them, day after day, and continue to reinforce an obsessive concern with your health, which is likely to lead to more dis-ease.

If, on the contrary, you wish to know how to be healthy, then be with healthy people. Or, if you want to know how to feel better about yourself, be with people who have high self-esteem. If you want to quit doing drugs or alcohol, stay around people who are sober. Don't spend all your time with people who share your limiting beliefs.

DREAMING

When you begin to examine and change your beliefs, another area of importance is your dreams. Pay attention to your dreams, keep a dream journal, and write down all the dreams you can remember. Realize that dreams are one of nature's therapeutic tools and begin to use your dreams to work out conflicts, explore old limiting ideas and take on new positive ones.

Every night before sleep, take five or ten minutes and focus on the issues that you want to resolve through your dreams. Imagine the ways that you want to change, and the new ways that you want to feel about yourself. Imagine the limiting beliefs that you want to lose dropping away in your dreams, the unresolved conflicts being worked out. Trust yourself, trust your dreams, and trust this natural healing process. In the morning, write down your dreams, and as you write them, allow yourself consciously to understand their meaning and to heal old difficulties and limitations.

JOURNALING

If you have beliefs that are blocking your emotional awareness and limiting your ability to feel alive and joyful, try keeping a daily journal. In this journal learn to express all your feelings of which you are aware. Past or present doesn't matter. Write fifteen or twenty minutes daily. This journal is only for you to see. It is not to be shown to others. Keeping this in mind keeps you from "writing for an audience." The point of this journal is for you to take the emotions from the *inside* and get them on the *outside.* That way you can see how your emotions, ideas, and beliefs fit together and understand how you have been limiting your experience by blocking your emotions.

When you use your daily journal, allow yourself to write without worrying about grammar, sentence structure, or spelling; it doesn't even have to make sense. This is an exercise in beginning to get to know the "inside" you from the "outside" you. By examining your innermost feelings in the light of your conscious awareness, you'll begin to see that many of your emotions that you thought of as unacceptable or unchangeable are actually created by old ideas and beliefs that can be changed. At times you will experience a realization of how old beliefs and old descriptions of yourself continue to create hidden emotions that become evident as you write. By putting them on the paper and seeing them clearly, you are able to begin to evaluate these emotions, accept them, and allow them to be released.

CATHARSIS

Another way of dealing with constricted emotions is to learn to express them in ways that do not harm you or another person. One of the problems that we create for ourselves is that as we repress our emotions over and over, we become a "pressure cooker" full of steam. Instead of learning how to open the petcock and let the steam out, we continue clamping the lid down tighter and tighter. At some point the lid will not clamp down any longer, the pressure cooker explodes and makes a "mess of the kitchen." In other words, at some point, we can no longer contain the suppressed emotions and we release them or "act them out" in ways that cause us to criticize and repress them further.

To learn to trust yourself and your emotions, you need to begin to express them in ways that you don't then judge. When you are feeling angry, irritated, or resentful, express the resentment or irritation before it builds into a rage. If you express these feelings daily, they don't have a chance to build. By learning to say, "I'm really disappointed that we had an agreement and you didn't keep the agreement", you will not repress your anger and later fly into a rage. You will not break things or attack other people. The anger and irritation will be expressed appropriately, day after day, before it becomes uncontrollable. By suppressing angers and resentments, either old or new, we eventually create what we most fear. We lose control of ourselves, and we act out in destructive ways that then cause us to judge our emotions once again.

There are many ways to express anger or other powerful emotions safely. We can yell and scream and hit a punching bag until we feel better. We haven't hit another person, we haven't hurt ourselves, and we have taken one more step towards learning that emotional expression is actually good and not to be feared. By practicing the expression of our emotions in appropriate ways, we learn not to judge our feelings. We learn to trust our emotions and accept them. When feeling sad, we can learn to let ourselves break down and sob. We won't die, we won't go crazy, people won't leave us. All the things we have feared all our life *will not happen.*

Another simple way to accept ourselves through expressing our feelings is to tell them to the people around us, and risk and trust that they're not going to judge us. By having good friends to whom we can express ourselves, we learn to accept ourselves and our emotions in ways we never believed possible. When we trust ourselves enough to express our feelings to another person and we don't see the judgment, anger, or rejection that we fear reflected back to us, we begin to realize that this fear of judgment comes from limiting beliefs often learned as children.

REFRAMING

Reframing means seeing the same situation in a different way. It is a powerful technique for changing our limiting beliefs and unwanted feelings. It is akin to the age old expression of seeing the glass either "half empty" or "half full."

For example, your spouse may say she is going to visit relatives for the weekend. At first you may look into the future and believe when this happens you will be alone, depressed, bored, and anxious. This will begin to create those unpleasant feelings now and encourage you to try and control him or her with pleading, manipulation, or anger. This typically leads to more unwanted feelings and conflict which reinforces more attempts at control causing additional stress.

Instead you can "reframe" the situation as an opportunity providing you with time to catch up on projects, get to know yourself, or visit friends you haven't seen in a long time. By doing this you suddenly feel good about the upcoming event which creates good feelings both in you and your mate. The same situation but a different view of it changes your entire experience.

There are many situations in life like this. A temporary layoff at work becomes an opportunity to spend more time with your children, an argument with a friend suggests a chance for a deeper communication leading to greater friendship, an illness becomes a time to assess your beliefs about your personal health and opens the way to increased vitality and strength. By seeing problems as challenges and opportunities, you reframe your daily experience and increase both your choices and personal freedoms.

In the future when faced with situations that you consider negative, take a few minutes to reconsider. What are some other ways of interpreting this situation? Which of these interpretations "feels" better? Then "step back" and see the situation from this "new" point of view. Allow yourself to feel what it feels like now. Act in accordance with this view. You have just reframed your experience and added to your daily choices. And, it feels better too!

BEGINNING THE JOURNEY

Belief therapy is about freedom. It is about understanding that each and every one of us creates our own individual reality. Understanding that we create that reality through our beliefs about reality. The only way to freedom and choice is through understanding, exposing and becoming aware of our limiting beliefs, and then changing them to create and reflect the reality we want.

Core beliefs are like powerful, unconscious "magnets" that attract clusters of smaller magnets. These smaller beliefs attract thoughts, ideas, and emotions, all related to the core belief. Somewhat like unconscious mental structures with their own fields of gravity and their own self-organizing principles. Once they are created and accepted as reality, they *become* reality.

One primary belief that all of us need to accept in order to clearly see the underlying limiting beliefs, is that beliefs *are changeable*. We do have *free will*, and we do create our own reality.

It is necessary that we understand and realize that we are not *born bad*. That whatever ideas, beliefs, or behaviors caused us to adopt a core belief of our badness, *it is not so.* All of us are born natural and free. We have a right to feel good about ourselves and to create the reality of our choice.

What I have attempted to do in this book is to give you permission to begin to explore the hidden beliefs that affect your daily experience. By seeing the power of beliefs, and by recognizing *your* power to challenge these beliefs, you will begin a process of change. A change towards freedom and personal responsibility. It is my desire that each of you examine your life through your behaviors, ideas, thoughts, and beliefs. By doing so, you will recognize, challenge, and change your limiting beliefs to create a life of quality and pleasure.

2

RELATIONSHIPS

*So you ask me, is it possible to lose something that was
not yours to begin with?
My answer is yes. For I have.
And in the grief I discovered that people cannot be kept
or told how they must be.
In the attempt of trying to create the perfect person you
unknowingly destroy that person who was your eternal
soul mate. And all the effort you put into changing this
person is actually only changing you.
And in the end leaving there together
two complete strangers
who don't even know themselves.*

Relationships are important to all living beings. We are social creatures. The old saying, "No man is an island" when read, "No man, woman, or child is an island", is in fact, *true*. Our entire civilization, culture, and social structure is based on cooperation with others of our kind. When you hear about "enlightened Gurus" living in the wilderness, in caves for 30 years, who write books and tell you how to live your life, *ignore them*. People who sit in a cave all their lives cannot even begin to tell other human beings how to live in a relationship.

Learning to live in relationship comes from being in relationship. Relationship requires certain skills that no one can learn in isolation. Relationship requires communication, which requires more than one person. It requires honesty with others, which requires more than one person. Relationship requires a willingness to open yourself up and to trust. Relationship requires a willingness to be vulnerable.

When people, because of their earlier experiences of betrayal, disappointment, and abandonment, choose to close off, distrust, and guard themselves from others, they become like that person living in isolation. They live in a cave of their own making; they live an impoverished life; they tell themselves it is better because they're safe. They may be safe, but the fact is that life isn't safe; life is to be lived, life is to be felt, and life is to be lived in relationship with others. It is impossible to be safe in a world where we all die anyway. You can create the illusion of safety by isolating yourself, but I promise you that there will come a time when your life will not be meaningful in isolation.

And when you find that your life is not meaningful, you're likely to reach out for meaning in another way, such as through drugs, alcohol, food, sexuality, or other compulsive behaviors.

People cannot live without other people, and yet to be in relationship means to be open and at times to be frightened and sometimes hurt. The simple fact is, while we have a high degree of control over our own life, we have virtually no control over the lives of others. And, we all have free will, which means those people that we care about and love, have the freedom to disagree with us, hurt us, leave us, or even die.

Often we try to find ways to resolve this fear of relationship with some defensive solution. One solution is an attempt to control the other, which creates dependency and co-dependency, which then leads to resentment, guilt, and impaired relationship. Another solution is to ignore the other person, pretend we don't care, and turn to addictions or other defenses to try to soothe our wounded feelings. Neither of these solutions are true solutions; they're short term solutions to long term problems. They cannot and will not work over time. A long-term functional relationship requires treating each other with respect and honesty, as well as a capacity to recognize our own helplessness and inability to control others. Relationship requires a degree of self-esteem and self-caring because if we don't believe in ourselves and trust ourselves, we will always be afraid that we are going to be abandoned since we feel we are unlovable. It requires being trustworthy because if we cannot trust ourselves, we will assume the other person is not trustworthy and we will be suspicious, insecure, and jealous of their love. It requires patience since we have all been brought up with limiting ideas and beliefs about ourselves and our world, that cause distress and insensitivity toward others.

We are social beings at biological, physical, emotional, and spiritual levels. People need people. And people who say they don't, have simply learned to deny that need, usually due to old issues like betrayal, distrust, or loss of friendship.

Staying alone, while you may not risk being hurt, you will in time come to feel empty and wonder, "Is this all there is?" Believing that you can successfully exist in isolation is delusional. Often people try to fill that isolation with work, pets, or hobbies. While some of these activities are important, and add to our pleasure and enjoyment; without others, these activities will eventually become dull and leave us with a need and longing for companionship and intimacy.

There is more than one kind of relationship. There are relationships with our children, which are not the same as relationships with adults; there are relationships with our boss, or other authority figures, which are different than our intimate relationships with those that we love. There are loving relationships with others that are non-sexual and there are sexual relationships with others that are also intimate and loving. Each one of these relationships has its own requirements and responsibilities, and each one of these relationships has the potential to be dysfunctional and destructive.

LOVE

What is love? Your concept of love will be influenced by how your parents treated each other. Did your parents yell and scream at each other? Did they call each other names? Did they hurt each other physically? Then your ideas about love are going to be colored by those destructive and abusive behaviors. You are going to be unsure about whether love means physical violence, screaming and yelling, or disrespect, and insensitivity.

Perhaps, on the other hand, your parents never yelled at each other, never fought, but also never expressed open affection? Did they act like strangers in the same house, or like acquaintances that happened to share the same bedroom? Did you seldom hear them saying "I love you", see them hugging and kissing, or walking hand in hand? Again, your concept of love is going to be guided by these early experiences and perceptions of your parents. In a home without overt affection, you are likely to believe that love is unemotional, intellectual, and boring because you were not exposed to the excitement, passion, joy, and exuberance of intimate adult love.

Or, perhaps, you were brought up in a family where your parents openly said that they loved each other, walked hand in hand, and greeted each other with a kiss and a hug. A family with parents that looked into each other's eyes with excitement and joy. If they were honest and loyal and exuberant in their love for one another, then your concept of love is going to include excitement, openness, and desire. If you were brought up in a family like that, count yourself fortunate. Those of us that were not, need to closely examine our beliefs about relationship to learn to create exciting, fulfilling, intimate, mature, loving, adult relationships.

FRIENDSHIPS

In this culture, we struggle with friendship. For example, there are many taboos regarding male same-sex relationships. To be close to another male is often viewed suspiciously. Strong feelings towards someone of the same sex commonly raises questions of sexual orientation. Does friendship necessarily have to imply romantic or sexual inclinations towards the other person? Of course not.

Often, with men, core ideas of competition create a need to put other men down in order to make themselves seem greater. Men compete for the best jobs, the most desirable women, and the most amount of money. This competition has forced men to suppress and deny their natural feelings of comradeship and look at themselves and others suspiciously when strong feelings are displayed. This is not true in all cultures. In the Italian culture, for example, men are expected to hug and kiss and to have a rich emotional life with each other. Here we tend to deny feelings of friendship, fraternity, and camaraderie which leads to an impoverished inner emotional life.

If two male or female friends spend the weekend together, fishing, shopping, or whatever, people wonder if there is something "wrong." Are they arguing with their spouse, going through some emotional crisis, or perhaps they have a sexual encounter planned. It is a sad situation when we are unable to feel natural feelings of love and caring without feeling ashamed. It's as if there is something "not quite right" about these feelings.

Women in this culture are usually taught to compete with other women for men. What happens to female relationships when women view other women as their competitors? The thoughts go like this: "Is she prettier?", "Is she thinner?" "Does he like her more?" This competition creates guardedness, distrust, and loneliness. Women who are secure enough to curb their competitive feelings are more comfortable in same sex relationships. And they are able to express emotion more easily with other women without fearing any sexual connotation.

In many other cultures, these taboos are not as strong. For example, in Mexico, adult women often walk down the street holding hands. Nothing is thought of this. In our culture, it's okay to be friends, but let's not "push it" with the "physical stuff" or people will start looking with sideways glances and judgment in their eyes.

Why should men have to be the biggest and the baddest, jump higher, run faster, be smarter, or have more money than other men in order to be considered worthy? Why should women have to be slimmer, younger, prettier, more seductive, and more sexual than other women to feel adequate and lovable? *They shouldn't.* These are limiting ideas that have been created from limiting beliefs based on misguided concepts, reinforced over years and years.

Once again, to change these limiting ideas, we must examine our core beliefs. Are we afraid of homosexual feelings? Do we believe friendship means that we are thinking in sexual ways? Is there something wrong with homosexual feelings? The idea here is choice. These judgments are limiting beliefs and behaviors that block us from emotional intimacy with ourselves and with others.

Even more difficult in this society is opposite-sex friendships. When a married person has a significant intimate relationship with someone of the opposite sex, they often risk divorce. It is clearly taboo. People at work are gossiping, the rumors are spreading, and the idea that you could actually be close friends with someone and *not* have a sexual relationship is almost unheard of. Expressions like "Where there's smoke, there's fire", "Did you see the way they looked at each other?" or "What do you think they're doing after work?" are commonplace.

True, in a society like ours, with many sexual hang-ups, it does take energy, consideration, and discipline to carry on opposite sex friendships without them becoming influenced by sexuality. But, that's all beliefs again! There's no reason that we cannot have deep, rewarding, intimate relationships with people of both sexes and still maintain a monogamous relationship with our spouse or significant other. This is not impossible, or even difficult. These are limited beliefs we've been taught to accept as reality. Choose the friends you want, examine the limiting beliefs that keep you from these friendships, and change them to beliefs that promote a life filled with companionship.

3

PARENTING

So what's it mean to be a parent
can't you see their frozen eyes
accepted into everything and left
with a path of lies
Can't you see your children's frozen eyes
Shown how to feel good but no one ever
told us what it was like to feel bad
Left alone so sad, oh Daddy, please
don't let my life just be a lie
Too soon, too quick, must learn to fly
Too soon, too quick, don't let me die.

What is a parent? For the last twenty-five years I've worked with sexually, physically, and emotionally abused children. They have often been taught that they have no value or self worth; that "love" equates to anger and violence. Currently, I have a 20-year-old patient, whose mother taught him to do intravenous heroin when he was 13 years old. She "jumped" him into a gang at about the same age. She beat him with a frying pan when he did not "behave." This patient is now in a treatment home for drug addiction and has been involved in drive-by shootings and stabbings. He weighs 220 pounds, is 6' 1", and acts like a little boy with no concept of what the world is about. His mother, to this day, continues to call the treatment home telling him to come back, where she and all his brothers and sisters still use heroin.

This patient says, "I want to see my mother, but I really want to be sober." He says to me, "I'm starting to like you, so be careful because I hit people I like." Around women he makes lewd and sexually inappropriate comments, and when confronted on his behavior, he says, "I really am sorry, I was only trying to express that I find you attractive."

This young man has been taught throughout his life to associate love with violence and to associate sex with degradation and abuse. When I say to him that he needs to stop all contact with his biological mother, he says, "But I can't, she's my mother." And I say to him, "Yes, she is your biological mother, but she is not, nor has she ever been, your parent."

Anyone can be a biological mother or father, all that is required is the sex act. And that is pretty easy to do—about as easy as falling down a slippery hill. So, why should special credit be given to people because they are a biological mother or a biological father? *It shouldn't.* We don't owe loyalty and respect because two people have sex. What we do owe loyalty, respect, and love for is parenting.

Parents are people who love and respect their children, and are able to put their own feelings aside to teach their children how to love and respect themselves. Parents are the ones who demonstrate love and respect in appropriate ways, who teach children self-love, self-respect and who teach their children consideration for others by being considerate of their children. A parent is a title that is *earned.* It is not a title that is given simply through sex.

Parenting is society's most valuable role. Parents teach their children how to think, how to act, and how to be in this world. Mothers and fathers who teach their children disrespect, hatred, and degradation are not only harming their children, but they are harming their children's children and everyone they are in relationship with. For us to survive, and for our children, grandchildren, and great-grandchildren to survive, we have to learn to treat ourselves and others with love and sensitivity. This must be taught in the young child's home. And that means it must be taught first and foremost by the parents, and the parents must take that responsibility as the most important obligation they have had the opportunity to perform.

Parenting must be taken seriously. That's not to say there should be no joy in parenting. It is one of the most joyful activities a person can do. Joyfulness, playfulness, exuberance, and zest for life are all ingredients of a good parent. So is respect for yourself as a person, and for your child. This respect is often demonstrated by setting appropriate limits and guidelines which requires caring enough to say "no" and caring enough to say "yes" and knowing the *difference* between the two. A healthy parent has the wisdom to know when it's appropriate to set a guideline and when it's appropriate to allow freedom. This takes understanding, self-awareness, and concern for that small person for which you are responsible.

The only true victims in life are children and 95 percent of the victimization of children happens within the home environment. *Parent* is an earned title, one that requires commitment and responsibility to yourself and your children, and one that you should be proud to have.

WHAT IS GOOD PARENTING?

They have a saying in recovery programs; "Keep It Simple Stupid." The way I think about "Keep It Simple Stupid" in terms of parenting is this: There is *no* particular parenting technique that is *right* and there is *not* one system that is better than another; but, there are things that are *wrong*. If you think of parenting as a continuum, with some parents allowing their children to do whatever they want, and other parents not allowing their children to do much of anything, you have the range. Almost anything in the middle is workable. However, there are a few requirements. First, is that both parents agree. A very disruptive element is for children to see their parents disagreeing on parenting. This situation allows the child to enter the adult relationship and creates "triangulation." The child has become involved in the parent's relationship and is forced to side with one parent or the other. Consequently the parents fight with each other over the child. This gives the child too much power, too much responsibility, and not enough guidance, which causes anxiety, omnipotence, grandiosity, and a lack of respect for authority.

As long as the parents avoid extremes and are in agreement, parenting is workable. You can be more conservative than the "average" parent, with a little more structure and guidance, or you can be more liberal, allowing more freedom than the "average" parent. Remember to agree with each other, listen to each other, talk to each other, and be reasonably consistent without being *rigid*.

No parent is perfect. This is an art that requires patience, balance, understanding, and above all, continuous communication and consistency. The parenting philosophy is less important than the consistency and the communication between two parents. It is essential that parents remain a team and that the children see the parents as "the parents" and the ones who are in charge of the household. This allows the children to relax, easing their anxiety about who is in charge and giving them direction at a time when they desperately need it.

It is not nearly as important whether that direction comes from a more conservative or liberal view point as it is that the direction exists and is consistent and that both parents are in reasonable agreement with it. This prevents triangulation and prevents the children from disrupting the parental relationship and the husband/wife intimate relationship. This also allows for consistency, guidance, and a foundation for children to grow and learn.

As the former clinical director of a program for emotionally disturbed children, I supervised the teachers and staff responsible for these children. These children had severe emotional problems and were very difficult to work with. Of the four classrooms I was responsible for, two worked quite well, and two didn't. One of the classrooms was run in a rather authoritarian way by a strong teacher that said, "This is my classroom and you're going to do it my way and that's the way it is", but he did it in a context of respect, care, and concern. There was mutual consistent respect between the children and teacher and his classroom worked.

In the second "working" classroom, children learned self-respect and other-respect. They continued to improve and progress in their education, both emotionally and academically. This teacher, however, was quite liberal and non-authoritarian, allowing her students much more freedom, but still within the context of respect, sensitivity, and caring. Again there was consistency above all. While her classroom may have been less structured than the other one, it was the same every day. The children knew it and they depended on it, and everybody in the classroom worked together to create that same environment. These children also worked well together, and continued to improve.

The third teacher just couldn't decide how she wanted to run her classroom. One week shc'd have one system, thc next week she'd have another system, and the week after, she'd have a third system. She kept looking for the magic formula for parenting or teaching, and *there is none.* Her classroom was constantly chaotic and out of control. She would say to us, "Well, look how out of control my classroom is, I need a new system." It didn't occur to her that she needed to be consistent and pick one system to follow through with. She kept switching techniques over and over, creating confusion and chaos in her room throughout the entire year.

In the fourth classroom, we rarely had the same teacher for any length of time. Due to the difficult population, teachers were always leaving. A new teacher would start to feel overwhelmed after a month and leave. That left the kids with a substitute in the class, then another teacher who would also get overwhelmed and eventually leave. That classroom was also chaotic, out of control, and damaging to the children.

You can think about these classrooms as four different family situations. The first teacher is like a mother and father[1] who are rather conservative. They have respect for themselves, respect for their children, and are consistent in their parenting. They have a well-run household with well-mannered children who learn to behave appropriately and respectfully.

The teacher in the second classroom is like the parenting figures who believe in a rather loose, unstructured situation, but they are still consistent in their communication and respect for each other. Though the children have more freedom than the average child, they know there are guidelines and boundaries and that their parents care enough to stop them from inappropriate behavior. Again, there is consistency and agreement between the parents.

[1] When I say mother and father, I'm talking about parenting figures. They may be step-parents, live-in parents; or single parents who have learned to use resources, such as friends or relatives, to back themselves up with the parenting.

Now, in the third household, like our third classroom, we have the parent figures who are changing the rules every week. One week they're doing it this way, the next week they're doing it that way. Nothing ever seems to stay the same. These parents are constantly looking for new plans, new parenting techniques, never staying with one parenting strategy long enough for it to work. The parents fight with each other over which technique is the better one, and consequently, the children are running wild. There is constant chaos and the children lack respect for themselves and others.

The fourth classroom situation, with multiple new teachers, is similar to a household where there are no consistent parenting figures. Every week there is a new man-friend or a new woman-friend, a new cousin or a new uncle, and these children never know who is going to be their "parent for the week." The father arrives, then leaves, or the mother comes in, and she leaves. The parents are splitting up every few months, followed by a time of living together for a few months. In this situation you have no consistency, no stability, and *no way* for these children to get appropriate parenting. You have chaos and lack of respect for all parties concerned.

These last two systems *do not work.* It is necessary that you have a dependable, consistent plan where the parenting figures listen to each other and their children, and where there are appropriate guidelines and freedoms.

Healthy parenting eliminates many children's problems that often are diagnosed with psychiatric labels, such as; attention deficit disorder, adjustment disorder, conduct disorder, and emotional disorders like depression and anxiety. Much of the time, these "disorders" are symptomatic of a lack of consistent parenting.

In a family where there are no limits, children grow up feeling omnipotent, all powerful, with no respect for authority and no respect for society. This results in acting out, oppositional behaviors. Sometimes this leads to anti-social personality disorders with violent and criminal behaviors.

In a family system where there are no privileges and children are over-controlled, they grow up rigid, overly-compliant, and lacking in creativity. They often reach adolescence only to rebel, being appropriate and well-behaved only when in the presence of the particular dominant parent. When that parent is absent, they run wild because they have been over-controlled.

In a family where the rules are always changing and the parent figures are always changing, children grow up confused, anxious, and insecure. They are often afraid of change and live fearful, guarded lives, denying their feelings. They are afraid to feel and afraid of emotional contact with others.

BELIEFS AND PARENTING

The beliefs that we are raised with, and that were modeled by our parents, are likely to determine much of our own parenting techniques. Generally speaking, there are core beliefs that underlie our concepts about parenting do's and don'ts. One core belief, that often develops, derives from our belief that our parents were good parents. Every child believes that Mommy and Daddy are heroes of one form or another. Daddy's the best painter, bricklayer, or scientist and Mommy's the best housekeeper, factory worker, or doctor.

Consequently, we brag to other children and ourselves about our parents, thereby insuring that we will adopt their beliefs, ideas, and behaviors, with little consideration as to whether these are appropriate or inappropriate beliefs. We then later model our own parenting techniques after them with little conscious awareness that we are doing so.

Often, this leads to polarization and extremes, very much like what we are trying to avoid. Our hypothetical parents are two adults, modeling their parenting after the way that they were parented, by four other parents, who were basing their parenting on their parents, that were raised by parents who were basing their parenting on their parents...ad infinitum. This leads to mass confusion wherein the parenting figures (which often includes multiple parenting figures like; uncles, aunts, step-parents, grandparents, and others) are responding to their own unconscious childhood beliefs that their parents modeled and which are usually in conflict with each other.

It's no wonder the children are confused when the parents are so confused. Consistency and balance are the necessary missing ingredients. Beliefs, ideas, and modeling behaviors of our own parents need to be examined. We then determine what we believe about these parenting techniques and how they influence our own parenting style. And next, as aware, conscious, adults with free will, we determine how to parent our children. Not based on our great-grandparents, grandparents, or parents, but based on what we believe to be appropriate, caring, loving, and consistent parenting.

To be "good enough" parents, it is essential that you recognize that there are no perfect parents, there are no perfect children, and that children are influenced by much more than just the parenting figures. Children come into the world with distinct ways of organizing behavior. Psychological studies demonstrate even infants have special likes and dislikes. Research indicates they will suck on a nipple to change television stations, and they have particular preferences in which programs they choose to watch. This suggests that even from birth we are to some extent individuals with certain likes and dislikes. Then, we take whatever we learn in the form of beliefs and other influences and organize them in particular and unique ways to create our own self.

There are many more influences on the child than their parents. With an extended family we have siblings, grandparents, aunts, uncles and cousins, all of whom have their own ideas and beliefs, which will have specific influences on a child. Also, the child forms friendships and is greatly influenced by these as well. His or her friends are often espousing totally different ideas, concepts, and beliefs than the family. The child's friend's parents may think very differently than his or her own parents, and now the child is exposed to a whole new set of beliefs and ideas.

At the age of five or six, the child goes to school where he or she is again exposed to a new set of ideals, beliefs, and concepts presented by the teacher. We know teachers are just people, but, the child looks at the teacher as an all-knowing authority figure, a role model who knows right from wrong, and knows how the child is supposed to think and act. The teacher hopefully takes this role seriously and believes their role is to teach the child how to think and act in society. Yet, each teacher has his or her own set of influences from their own childhood.

Consequently, we have teachers who all have varying ideas about how children should think, feel, or behave. The teacher's ideas become powerful influences on the child, and they are often as inconsistent and contradictory as the ideas of the parent. Also, teachers change quite frequently. We have substitute teachers and new teachers every year. If parents move around, there are multiple teachers in any given year, each of which have many different effects on the child's early belief system.

Another very powerful influence is mass-media. The child, from a very young age, is exposed to a variety of influences on television. These range from extremely violent cartoons, to daily news, to various types of sitcoms and dramas representing a variety of ideas, most of which are not ones that we would really want to engender in our young children as core beliefs. Consider the normal content of a week of television in your home. Think for a moment of the degree of intelligence, sophistication, personal responsibility, and caring that is demonstrated by the average half-hour sitcom or talk show on daytime or evening television. Then consider that our children are listening to these influences many hours per week.

Last but not least, our children have interests of their own. A primary one is music, which is often listened to through headsets so there are no other distractions. They then turn the volume up to an astounding degree and consequently the lyrics are pounded into their psyche hour after hour, day after day, week after week, year after year. They often go to sleep at night with this influence still pounding into their brain. *Talk about hypnosis!* What a powerful hypnotic technique, to hook up young children (who have not yet developed their own adult concepts of the world) and expose them to repeated powerful messages that are drummed into them in a rhythmical, musical format. Often the *messages* are hardly even acknowledged, let alone examined, due to the influence of the musical rhythm or score. What an ideal way to brainwash a population. And yet our children volunteer for this brainwashing on a daily basis. They don't consider the long-term effects of this behavior and adults are often too busy or too unaware to consider these influences.

Read the lyrics of most of the music that children listen to these days. I personally enjoy music and think of it as a wonderful form of artistic expression, body awareness, and emotional stimulation. However, I cannot deny the powerful impact that *any* ongoing consistent message, is going to have when it is forced into the emerging minds of our youth in such a dramatic way. Therefore, it is important to at least ask the question, "What exactly are they listening to?" and "How is it likely to effect them?"

To restate my point, children, from the time they are born, have a multitude of influences besides parenting. While parenting influences are certainly important, and one of the primary ways that children's ideas and beliefs are shaped, there are many other powerful methods that help children form perceptions about reality. And, as they emerge from adolescence to adulthood, regardless of what those influences are, our children, just like ourselves have free will... the ability, obligation, and responsibility to direct these different influences in whatever way they choose. But, to be able to use influences appropriately, they need to see the hidden beliefs that they have been brought up with. Otherwise, those beliefs are misinterpreted as reality and become unconscious. Then, rather than examine and change these beliefs, these perceptions are considered reality. Once we have accepted core beliefs as reality, they determine our feelings, thoughts, and behavior. We are no longer free and we no longer exercise choice. We are then responding to core beliefs about reality as if they were reality, and it does not occur to us that we can change our ideas, beliefs, and "reality."

Viewing child rearing in this framework, it becomes clear that while each parent is responsible for doing the best they can to help promote healthy ideas and beliefs in their children, their influences are only a part of the picture. To be "healthy" each person has to be aware ultimately of the biases they have been exposed to and examine those biases from a perspective of adult awareness and intelligence, then make choices about how they are going to live their own life.

As parents, once we've done what we can, it is time to recognize that we can no longer control our children and that it is time for them to be adults and to control themselves. That being the case, we are no longer responsible for our adult children's behaviors and it is incorrect to hold ourselves overly responsible for their early childhood. We do the best we can, recognizing there are a multitude of influences in becoming an adult, and ultimately we recognize that our adult children are responsible and free adults, as we ourselves are.

4

ABUSE AND TRAUMA

Blood soaked blankets cover my body
inside this cold pine box
Dried up layers of soil and rock
seal the seams of my thought.
Laughing memories of clowns in my head
Scarcely marching in the circus of the dead.
Cry you lonely ones, cry from your watery eyes
Cry you broken child, cry from the bed in which you lie!

Extremely abusive and traumatic events in our lives create *powerful* core beliefs, somewhat like "black holes" in the psyche. We avoid them at all costs, and yet because we avoid them, we keep getting sucked back in, feeling lost, frightened, crazy, and out of control. This chapter is about powerful life experiences of sexual, physical, or emotional abuse that have created frozen moments in our psyche. We attempt to defend ourselves from these "abuse moments" with all the addictive and obsessive behaviors available to us. We run from these feelings at all costs and in any way possible.

To heal these powerful events and create comfort in our lives, it is necessary to quit running. It flies in the face of reason to go back into these deep, crippling areas of abuse, and yet we *must*. Some of us have experienced daily sexual, physical, and emotional trauma, until we believed that we had absolutely no value and felt we could die at any moment. These are very difficult problems to work out, and yet without resolving them, we continue to be controlled and victimized by our past.

The way to heal trauma is no different than any other conflicted area of our life, with one possible exception. Those of you with experiences of deep abuse or trauma may not be able to expose them, accept them, and release them by yourself. You may need the help of a third party. A caring, supportive, knowledgeable helper. Whether that person be a therapist, teacher, or friend, they will need expertise and ability to aid in the healing of abuse and trauma.

Whoever it is, make sure you have trust in them. They need to be trustworthy with these issues you're about to expose. When you begin this process, you may feel like you're slipping and losing yourself. You may feel a threat to your very identity. You may feel like you are going to die, go crazy, or disappear, never to come back again. At those times you need a friend or companion. You need a *guide*. This journey takes time and it takes courage. Think of it as an exploration to an unknown land. You never know for sure what's over the next hill or around the next corner. You know you are frightened but you also know that the only way that you can explore, learn about, and eventually tame the unknown, is by going through this process.

The truth is, the feelings locked up in abuse and trauma are no more dangerous than feelings locked up in small difficulties. They're still only "paper dragons." They do not have the power to kill you, make you go crazy, or make you kill others. However, they have been repressed so long that they feel overwhelming and more powerful than they really are. For example, the rage and fear connected with trauma *is* more intense than feelings associated with lesser events. But, they have no more *power* than any other feelings. They are just feelings. Powerful feelings, intense feelings. Think of them as very bright, vivid colors that have to be examined and accepted in order for the healing process to take place. It is by going through these feelings that we find the core beliefs connected with them. Beliefs we have integrated into our core self that are connected to feelings of fear, rage, isolation, despair, and even self-destruction. Often these old beliefs, represented in the form of self-talk, sound like this: "I'd rather be dead than face this", "I'll do anything to get out of this", "I can't handle this; nothing matters anymore."

The beliefs and ideas connected with traumatic feelings are often at the heart of suicidal thoughts and behaviors. We *believe* that death is the only way out. *It's not! Life is the way out.* But the only way through life is through these feelings. *No* feeling can make you kill yourself. *No* feeling can make you harm someone else. But the fear of these emotions is intense, and is best experienced with a guide. Someone that understands you, is supportive of you, and is willing to allow you to feel your feelings. Someone who has explored and worked through their own deep emotions, so they don't run at that very moment when you most need them to be there.

The process of healing is exactly the same for deep trauma as for lesser problems. We expose the core beliefs that are connected with the abuse and trauma. We learn that the people that have traumatized us are no longer able to do that. As adults we can protect ourselves and stop any present or future abuse. We no longer need to avoid these old feelings or place ourselves in similar abusive circumstances in a misguided attempt to somehow fix the past. There is nothing to fix except learning to care for and trust yourself. *This you can do!*

At times during this process, it will seem that you've gone down into a dark, dark cave and that you can't see the light behind you or the light in front of you. It feels as if it's too late to go back and you're afraid to go forward. These are powerful feelings, but still only feelings. This is normal and natural and expected.

You need to continue to move forward. At some point you will again experience the light and find your way to firm footing. It's like crossing a swamp to get to the other side; it's a transitional period. Sometimes it feels like the earth is moving underneath your feet and likely to swallow you up. But the truth is, there are no real alligators in this swamp, it does not have quicksand, and it is shallow enough to trudge through. It won't be easy, it won't be fun, but you can do it and it is worth doing. This is the point at which you will no longer be haunted by these past experiences of abuse and trauma that have influenced your life for so long.

5

CODEPENDENCY AND DEPENDENCY

*Sent a message with a draft that blew through my here.
Collected fragments of your there with only imagination.
Left my here to only find you standing there in hopes of
something different. Now I find myself only standing
right beside you. Why is nothing different?
I left my here to find you there and it's as though I never
left. Could well be that some speech or movement might
help us leave. But if that's so, still where would we be?
I feel the need of some sort of in between where placement is with -
out importance and my place would be in me.*

A codependent is someone who needs to take care of someone else in order to feel secure and safe that the other person will not leave them or abandon them. They need the other person to value them, love them, and meet the codependent's hidden and unspoken needs. Codependency, on the face of it, often looks altruistic but codependency creates dis-ease in both the codependent and the dependent, and codependents have one of the most difficult addictions to give up.

The reason that codependency is difficult to give up is because the codependent is valued. Codependents always do more than their share. They are concerned, and caring. They're there whenever you need them, and they look like they can carry the weight of the world on their back. They typically look like they've got it all together. They appear to be strong and willing to serve in any form or capacity necessary.

Here's a familiar example: On a bad day at the office, after just having a fight with your spouse, a codependent says, "What's wrong with you, honey?", "Is there anything I can do?", "Can I get you a glass of water?", "Do you want to talk about it?", "Do you need some time off?" Or, if you don't have a job and you're really not looking for one and you're basically not taking responsibility for yourself because you are busy blaming everyone else, there's comfort in hearing a codependent say, "It really is their fault, you're doing the best you can," "Let me help you," "I can loan you another ten dollars", "I can buy you diapers for the baby," or "I'll help you look for a job."

Codependents are usually very bright, always have the answer, always know what's right for somebody else, and are always willing to go the extra mile. Codependents, in this society, get rewarded. They are looked up to and appreciated. They get the promotions because they are always doing more work than their co-workers. They get the approval because they are there when you need them. Codependents are like the hub of a wheel and all the spokes go out to the dependents. Around every true codependent you'll find several dependents that believe that their survival is dependent on the codependent. And, likewise, the codependent, also believes that the dependent would not survive without them.

You see this pattern in dysfunctional and destructive relationships. The wife of an alcoholic says, "I can't leave him, he'll kill himself if I do" and she continues to suffer. She is constantly complaining that she carries the burdens of the world on her shoulders. You see this in the spouse who says, "I have to pay all the bills, work all day, take care of the kids, take care of the house, *and* take care of the dependent. If I don't do it, who will?"

You also see this in the codependent father whose adult children never get a job, or if they do, only keep it for a week. But still, Daddy's always there with the extra five or the extra twenty or the extra hundred to take care of the weekend date, the grandkid without diapers, or the electricity that was just turned off. Usually because his adult children went out for an expensive dinner and then couldn't find the money to pay the utilities.

Or, there are the long-suffering spouses, who put up with all kinds of irresponsible behaviors from their mate. Whether it's multiple affairs, alcoholism, drug addiction, or spousal abuse. The codependent is always suffering, always there, and always complaining about doing more than his or her share. Yet, no one looks closely enough to see that the codependent needs a dependent just as much as a dependent needs a codependent. This is like a hand-in-glove relationship. Each is *inter*dependent on the other. And, by definition, this is a *dysfunctional* relationship, ultimately doomed to fail.

Codependent/dependent relationships are based on mutual need, not on mutual desire. They're not based on two adults caring for one another and choosing to be in a

relationship with each other. They're based on two insecure adults who feel inadequate at the core. Both are
afraid of abandonment and both need each other in order
to fill the emptiness in them, and to quiet the fear of being
alone. That's primarily what the codependent and the
dependent have in common, a crippling fear of loneliness
and abandonment. They believe no one will be there if they
don't have each other to cling to.

This fear of abandonment is often related to early childhood trauma. The codependent, or the dependent, felt
abandoned by the mother, father, or other parenting figures. In the case of the codependent, the personality dys-
function typically begins when one or both parents are
unable or unwilling to take care of themselves. Alcoholic
parents, sick parents, psychotic parents, absent parents,
or single parents that befriend their small children and
make them emotional support for themselves are examples. These are parents who in some way need the child to
take care of them. This forces young children to push
aside their own feelings, rise above their needs, wants and
desires, and become "pseudo-adults", or small adults in a
child's body. This is necessary in order to keep the attention, approval, and love of the dysfunctional parent, or to
keep the parent from abusing them and abandoning them.
It is survival for these children to rise above their feelings
and do more than their share to meet the emotional
demands of the powerful but dysfunctional adult.

These demands may mean being emotionally available
for the alcoholic parent, nursing the sick parent, or being
pretty enough for the seductive parent. If the parent has
lost dreams from their own childhood, then the child may
be required to be the smartest one in the class or the
fastest one on the team. In some form or other, the small
child has to rise above their own needs and care for the
adult. This creates the emerging codependent drama. This
also evokes the codependents fears of abandonment,
rejection, and a pervasive sense of inadequacy, which con-
tradicts the codependent facade of, "I can do anything for
anybody."

Codependents need the dependent as much as the dependent needs them. And they believe if they set appropriate limits by saying "no", or if they quit doing more than their share, everybody is going to go away and they will be left alone. They believe they are not adequate enough, worthy enough, or desirable enough the way they are. They believe that in order to be loved, they must *always* walk the extra mile.

In every codependent, no matter how altruistic they seem, there is an underlying selfishness. Codependents need to take care of dependents because of their own fears, even if "taking care" of the dependent cripples the dependent and makes them unable to care for themselves. For example, the doting mother, who in fact needs the young child's attention and emotional support for herself, and consequently, infantilizes her child. She's chronically, obsessively concerned with her child's every move. They are never allowed to become a man or a woman because she needs them to be an infant forever in order to justify her own need. Sometimes you see this in mothers who adopt developmentally disabled children. This appears very altruistic, and certainly the child needs someone like this in their environment. But often the mother has adopted a baby, who can never be anything but a baby, out of her own fear of abandonment and rejection. This "child" will always need her. Now she has someone that she can control, love, and who she knows will love her forever. They cannot leave her as they are fully dependent on the parenting figure.

Codependents don't trust. They need to do more than their share because they don't *trust* that others will be there, unless they *do*. They are able to trust only as long as the dependent needs them. The problem is, even though they trust the dependent not to leave them, they never really trust that they are cared for or loved. This is because they always secretly believe that the dependent is only there because the codependent is doing more than their share. They believe as soon as they set appropriate limits or take care of themselves, the dependent will leave.

And, because they have found the opposite person, the dependent, to fill this dysfunctional system, this is often very true. When a codependent does begin to set limits, the dependent either has to grow up and become a responsible adult or they have to find another codependent to be dependent on. And they often find another codependent.

What creates a dependent? Codependents create dependents. A parent figure who does more than their share for their children are the same parents who need their children to need them. They are obsessively concerned with taking care of the minute details of the child's life: picking up the toys for the child, doing the chores for the child, or worrying excessively about the child's social life. As the child gets older, the parent continues to put up with their behavior without setting appropriate limits. Defending the child from natural consequences such as school problems, difficulties with peers, or in the work place, creates dependency. These parents are always available to defend and protect the child against outside forces, which creates in the child a belief that they need this protection and cripples their ability to care for themselves.

And, for the dependent, the "codependent" can be a friend, doctor, cult, church, hospital, or even a prison. It can be any authority that promises to meet their daily needs, so they are not required to grow up and function as an adult.

A current example of a codependent/dependent system is our extended welfare program. We pay people to have children, stay at home, and not work. And we pay them enough to where it is almost impossible for them, once they are dependent on the system, to leave it. To get a job that will pay them as much as they are making on welfare, and enough to pay for the child care required, is very difficult. The welfare system becomes the codependent to people's irresponsible dependency. And, although it is designed to help, like every codependent's conscious intent to help, what it does is cripple people and make them less able to care for themselves.

Another element of the codependent/dependent relationship is that the codependent feels they are not appreciated. The codependent believes that no matter how much they do, the dependent never really appreciates the suffering and sacrifice they are making. The truth is, they are right. The reason that they're right is because the dependent, while believing they need the codependent, unconsciously resents the codependent because they know that they are being crippled in the process. The dependent knows the only way they are going to be like other people is to learn to stand on their own and to be an adult.

Dependents know they have become dependent on others to care for them, and this contributes to low self-esteem. They resent those "others" and they blame them for their inadequacy. This is another thing that dependents and codependents have in common: the dependent blames the codependent for everything and the codependent agrees. The codependent takes more than their share of responsibility and the dependent takes less than their share of responsibility. You have an over responsible adult taking care of an under responsible adult. Unless the codependent stops doing this, or the dependent decides to grow up and refuses the help, this process can go on indefinitely. Both of them remain in a dysfunctional, unrewarding, and emotionally abusive relationship—neither able to live their own life. The codependent is chronically obsessed and concerned about the dependent, and the dependent always feels tied to the apron strings of the codependent.

CHANGE

Breaking the codependent/dependent spiral is an opportunity and a challenge for both. It is absolutely essential that one or the other break the spiral to stop the dysfunctional relationship.

This spiral is based on core *beliefs*. The core beliefs for the codependent are: "I need to do more than my share in order to be good enough", and "If I'm not good enough, people won't want me, they will leave me", and, "I will be utterly alone and abandoned. I would rather die than be utterly alone and abandoned." And for the dependent, the core belief is: "Others have to take care of me because I am not able to take care of myself", "I am too weak", "too inadequate", or "too sick." These core beliefs function at an unconscious level within the codependent/dependent spiral and tie together the dysfunctional and destructive relationship.

Codependency and dependency are addictions. *Powerful addictions!* More so because they are seductive, hidden, and unconscious, not even usually perceived as addictions. The codependent is viewed as a responsible and respectable member of society. They reap many rewards for their codependency, but inside they feel empty and alone. When the codependent is not feeling overwhelmed and resentful, they're feeling guilty because they're not doing enough. Underneath they wonder "Is this all there is?" But, they feel compelled to continue. They truly believe that if they do not take care of the dependents, the dependents will die. It becomes a life and death matter.

Dependents don't see codependency as an addiction because they genuinely believe that they *are* dependent on the codependent. They believe that they are not capable like other people, and they require and deserve a codependent to take care of them. Both parties fail to see clearly the dysfunctional and addictive spiral. This makes treatment difficult.

The first step in healing the codependent/dependent relationship is to acknowledge that it *is* truly a codependent/dependent relationship. One way for a codependent to know that a particular behavior is codependent, rather than genuine caring, is how they feel when they set appropriate limits on their helping. Can they sleep at night? Do they feel okay, even if the other person makes bad choices? Or do they continue to feel guilty and responsible for that other person? Do they recognize that people are responsible for themselves?

The expression, "You can lead a horse to water, but you can't make it drink", is analogous to leading dependents to water, if they don't drink, are you going to recognize that this is the choice of the dependents or are you going to continue to try and make them drink? Do you feel that you have failed if you can't? If so, that's codependency. If you buy people books and they tear out the pages, are you going to say, "Oh well, I did my share? If they don't want to read the book that's their choice." Or are you going to try and put the pieces of the book back together and read it to them? If you do, you're a codependent.

Codependents feel resentful, responsible, and guilty. They chronically do more than their share. In contrast, responsible adults often help, recognize the help may or may not be taken, only offer help given without attachment to the outcome, recognizing that if the help isn't taken there is no need to feel resentful or guilty.

Healing the codependent/dependent trap requires *see-ing* your role in the process, then changing it. If you are the codependent, you must set appropriate limits on your behavior. Quit doing more than your share. Learn to say "no." Learn to take care of yourself.

When you begin to change these behaviors, you will experience feelings that you don't like. These are the feelings that you have been trying to avoid by being a codependent. You will initially feel anxiety and guilt with this new experience. Not much better than the resentment and helplessness you feel while being a codependent. The difference is that with time these feelings will get better. Taking care of yourself is a solution, not a problem. As you learn to tolerate the guilt and anxiety, you will begin to realize that you don't have to do more than your share to be accepted. People don't have to need you in order to want you. Some people will leave, but others will come to take their place. These new relationships will not be based on a dysfunctional pattern. They will be based on mutual caring and equal responsibility. Other people in your environment will actually change when you quit taking care of them. Some of them will "grow up" and begin to function as adults. Those relationships will become more satisfying and rewarding for both of you.

This change in relationship will allow you to begin to trust yourself and others to a degree not possible before. The new trust and intimacy in your life will increase your self-esteem, leading to more trust and even better relationships. At last, with each change, the "snowball" is rolling the *right* way down the hill. You will find increased pleasure and quality in your life as you free yourself from your old codependent ways.

How do you recognize if you are functioning in a *dependent* way? Are you the one that often doesn't have a job? The one with the addictions? The one that always seems to need help? Do you often feel resentful when you don't get what you want? Do you often take more than your share and give less than your share? Then you are functioning in a dependent style and it is just as crippling as the codependent style. Even though it seems like it is working for you, it is not. It is based on low self-esteem, feelings of inadequacy, and a demand that everyone else owes you something. That's a miserable way to wake up in the morning and a miserable way to live your life. The solution is to recognize that this behavior is based on limiting core beliefs.

If you find yourself on the dependent side of the codependent/dependent trap, it is necessary to act contrary to your beliefs. You have learned to believe you are irresponsible and unable to take care of yourself. By *acting* responsible and independent, you prove to yourself those old beliefs are wrong. You prove that you are capable and responsible. This changes your limiting core beliefs and consequently changes your current reality. You begin to believe in yourself and others begin to believe in you also.

You find that you no longer *want* extra help from codependents because it makes you feel helpless and inadequate. You begin to know you are not helpless and inadequate, and you realize you are just as capable, worthy, and "response-able" as anyone. *Acting* response-able *creates* responsibility, ending the codependent/dependent curse and provides a life of increased quality and meaning.

6

ADDICTIONS

A Meeting With Myself

*I've finally reached the point where I've come to realize,
my past so wrong
Too many things I now can't change.
My problem's a brick wall blocking the path to a better life.
Now with nowhere to go anger
and total frustration burst within me,
as I go crashing through that wall
hoping to find everlasting
answers, but only to find another wall.*

What is an addiction? By my definition an addiction is a compulsive behavior accompanied by obsessive thoughts for particular substances or behaviors that we believe are necessary for our existence. We also believe that without these substances or behaviors, life would barely be worth living.

Another way to think about addictions is behaviors that are significantly harming our life in one or more areas and we continue them anyway. Drinking, in and of itself, is not an addiction. Drinking to the extent that you begin to have serious work, health, or personal problems is an addiction. Sexuality is not in and of itself a problem, but when the need to have sex is overpowering and it is accompanied by obsessive thoughts and compulsive behaviors, it is. These compulsive sexual behaviors often generate exploitive, limited, and brief relationships, leaving the persons involved empty and alone. I consider this addictive and dysfunctional behavior.

Enjoying good food and looking forward to an excellent meal is certainly not a bad thing, in fact it is part of a quality life. But if we find ourselves obsessively thinking about our next meal, eating faster than those around us, choosing certain places to go solely for the food, and placing ourselves at risk with extremes in weight, then our obsession with eating is dysfunctional and addictive and ultimately creates health and body image problems.

Gambling is not necessarily negative. To enjoy a game of poker or to occasionally visit Las Vegas or place a bet on your favorite sports team, may enhance your awareness and pleasure of the particular event. But when you find that you are unable to pay your bills, your spouse is ready to leave, and all you can think about is trying to figure out the angle on the next bet, you have a gambling addiction and it is limiting your life.

There are many, many kinds of addictions. If you are working ten, twelve, fourteen hours a day, six or seven days a week, you probably have an obsessive compulsive need to work. It is likely that you don't feel good about yourself unless you are working. Even activities that people think of as healthy, like running and exercising, can be overdone. If you are depressed because you missed one day of exercising or you discover that no matter how far you run, you need to run further, you may be overdoing it. When you begin to experience health problems from working out, or you can't enjoy other activities unless you've already done your work-out for the day, then you have an obsessive compulsive behavior that has gone beyond enhancing physical fitness.

What causes an addiction to be addictive? What is it that we are trying to do with our addictions? What are we trying to accomplish with obsessive, compulsive behaviors? Primarily we are trying to avoid or eliminate underlying feelings that we don't want to feel.

This is not to say that there is not a physiological component in certain addictions such as alcohol, heroin, or even nicotine. But, by the time the addiction gets rolling, there is both a physiological and psychological component which makes stopping that much more difficult. Anyone can be detoxed from alcohol, nicotine, or heroin within three days to three weeks. Once they're detoxed, they no longer have a *physiological* addiction. So, to call these substances physiologically addicting is only partly true. A great majority of people, even after detox and their body is chemically free from the substance, crave the substance and continue to go back into the addiction over and over. This demonstrates that these addictions are not as much physiological as they are psychological.

What is a psychological addiction if not an attempt to escape from unwanted feelings? If you can learn to tolerate any feeling, anytime, anywhere, then *you* choose your behavior and *you* choose what you're going to do on any given day. If you're unable or unwilling to tolerate your feelings, then you have no choice. You are no longer free and you *will* engage in obsessive compulsive behaviors, otherwise known as addictions or defenses, to block your unwanted feelings.

The problem is that the ability of addictions to block unwanted feelings is *temporary*. You can only smoke so many cigarettes, run so many miles, or have sex for so long. You can only drink so much alcohol and you can only do so many drugs. Eventually you're back, and not only do you have the old feelings, they're actually *worse* than they were before you began the obsessive compulsive behavior. Because now you have accompanying shame and guilt over the very behavior that was designed to get rid of the feelings. This becomes a spiraling effect, a snow-ball rolling down the hill the wrong way, a self-fulfilling prophecy. "I have this feeling I don't want, so I'm going to take this substance to get rid of it. Now that I've taken this substance to get rid of it, I feel guilty and ashamed over taking the substance because I know that this is causing problems in my life. So now I need to get rid of the feelings of guilt and shame, which leads to taking more substances which leads to...."

In essence, an addiction is a short-term solution to a long-term problem, but the solution itself becomes part of the problem. "I'm going through a divorce and I have feelings of abandonment, anger, and loneliness and so I take up drinking to get rid of the feelings. Now I'm drunk every night and I feel ashamed and guilty, and I still feel abandoned, angry, and lonely. Now that I'm drinking constantly, I'm even more abandoned and lonely because I'm isolating myself from others and others are isolating themselves from me. Now what do I do? Since I'm feeling even more ashamed, angry, guilty, abandoned and lonely, I need to drink more, which creates more of the same feelings, which creates more of the drinking." This eventually leads to self-disgust, depression, and seriously damaging addictive behavior.

What is the solution to these life-threatening problems? The solution is simple but true. We need to learn to tolerate, accept, and eventually to trust our feelings.

Our feelings mostly come from early core beliefs and ideas about ourselves that caused us to suppress our emotions. As children these were often truly overwhelming feelings. We felt that if we didn't suppress our anger, our parents may leave us, hurt us, or kill us. We believed that if we did express our loneliness, sadness, or fears, that others would judge us and leave us and we might die. There are many reasons why the feelings of our childhood were so overwhelming, and we were so unable to feel them and express them.

As children we often did need to suppress our strongest feelings. In some families, if a child speaks too much or too loudly with anger, he or she gets abused and hurt. In other families, if you cry, you may get beat up. If, every time a child speaks, he or she is told they are stupid and to shut up, they will suppress their feelings. All children need approval from the parenting figures. Therefore, parental judgment is frightening, and causes children to suppress emotions at all costs.

As adults we forget that we are no longer children, and we forget that our parents no longer have the power to hurt us, judge us, and to make us feel so alone and frightened. We don't realize that the feelings that have been repressed all these years have become like "paper dragons." It feels like they still have the power of a true dragon, but the truth is, they don't. If we learn to tolerate and accept our feelings, we will find that they no longer have power over our lives. They are only powerful due to old beliefs. An example of this kind of belief is, "If I tell people I'm angry, they'll hurt me"; "If I let people know that I'm scared, they'll ridicule, humiliate, and leave me."

The people who taught us these ideas are often no longer in our environment, and even if they are, they can no longer hurt us. The feelings that we're so afraid of expressing, developed from core beliefs that are no longer germane to our daily living situation.

Our defenses are like giant walls built around a castle when the barbarians were threatening to overrun it. The barbarians left many years ago, but the walls are so high that we've never bothered to climb up to the top and take a look to see if the barbarians are still out there. They are *gone,* the danger is over! While, the emotions may *feel* intense and uncomfortable, they are no longer a danger. Accepting this, we can learn to tolerate and accept our feelings and then make *choices.* These choices will not be based on the need to rid ourselves of feelings, but based on what we want for our lives. This is the only way our lives can have freedom and quality. Without the ability to tolerate our ongoing emotions we have no choices in our lives. Instead, we are always running from feelings, and running from the unconscious beliefs that are creating the feelings. This all comes from erroneous beliefs that our feelings are reality, and are dangerous.

No feeling, in and of itself, is dangerous. It is only the unexpressed, repressed feelings that build up like our pressure cooker. We attempt to keep the lid on by clamping it down tighter and tighter. But as anyone who has ever seen a pressure cooker knows, when the pressure begins to build, you don't clamp the lid down tighter. Instead open the petcock, turn down the fire, or get it off the burner.

When we close the lid tighter and tighter, when the feelings are repressed too long, the pressure cooker eventually "blows up" and we fly into some type of inappropriate behavior which "makes a mess of the kitchen." Feeling guilty and remorseful over this behavior, we then feel that it's necessary to continue to "clamp the lid down even tighter."

These are compulsive, self-defeating behaviors based on misguided ideas about the power of early childhood feelings. These feelings don't need to be given that power. We no longer need to run from them. We can, in the light of our conscious, everyday lives, make decisions based on what we choose to do, not based on what we need to do in order to avoid old feelings.

LOSING ADDICTIONS

Take some time to write down all your beliefs about your addictions. If you have an eating disorder, write down how you feel about food, write down how you felt as a child about food, write down what your mother and father told you about food. You may find that every time Mom felt good towards you and you felt accepted and loved by her, she gave you something sweet to eat. You connected love and approval with sweet food. Now when you're feeling alone and unloved you have this compulsive need to eat chocolate. This is really an unconscious connection with that early, learned behavior of love being synonymous with sweets. At an unconscious level, you believe if you eat enough cake, cookies, or candy that you're going to feel loved. The truth is you're *not*. You're going to feel disgusted, guilty, and ashamed of overeating. It no longer works. You're confusing the food or the substance with the love and approval of the mother or father. Only by seeing how you've made this erroneous connection between your childhood and your present life, can you change this behavior.

Let's examine other addictions like drinking alcohol or taking drugs. If you grew up in a family where every time Mom or Dad had a feeling they didn't like, they popped a pill or opened a beer, then what did you learn? What you learned was that any time you're uncomfortable with what you're feeling, take a substance. Or, if every time you had a slight pain or discomfort, Mom said, "Take this pill" or "Drink this medicine," you learned to medicate feelings and sensations. You learned the same on television; "If you don't like the way you are feeling, take two of these and call me in the morning." We have an entire society that has been hypnotized into believing they're not supposed to feel any discomfort or distress, and if they do, the way to get rid of it is to take some powerful, often unnatural substance into their body.

Watching your family take substances to change the way they felt taught you to do the same. It also taught you that, it's the *only* way to change how you feel.

ALTERNATIVES

If you're feeling sad or lonely, write down your feelings in a daily journal. Write down how you feel every single day until you feel better. If you're feeling like you're holding in too many feelings (like the "pressure cooker"), find useful ways to express them. Talk to a friend, get a punching bag and beat it, pound on a pillow and yell and scream until you feel better. Take up an art project, or a musical instrument, and use expressive techniques to get your feelings out.

When we feel that we need to take a substance in order to "medicate" our feelings, what this really means is we've got too many feelings all stuck together. We need to find ways to unstick them. We need to find ways that are not going to make us feel ashamed and that are not going to hurt us or anyone else. This way we don't judge the feelings and stuff them back in.

Think of feelings like *colors*. Blues, reds, greens, yellows or purples. These colors are not bad or good, but some are lighter, brighter, darker or more or less intense. Imagine feelings as *healing* colors, and realize that as you stay with that healing color, it begins to shift and move into another color, and another, and so on. By learning to talk about that "color" or express that feeling in some activity that does not harm yourself or others, you will learn to tolerate feelings not previously tolerated. Soon you will find that you can experience the identified feeling without the original discomfort.

With this technique you are learning to heal chronic, suppressed, frightening feelings from your past. As healthy adults, we learn to feel our feelings, sort them out, and look for the underlying beliefs that are creating them. We can then change these beliefs to more life-promoting ones. This allows us to lead freer quality lives as aware adults.

As you learn to accept your feelings and to not run away with compulsive addictions and behaviors, you'll find this process is not easy. We've had our entire life to judge our emotions and push them away. When you first begin to experience repressed feelings, they feel frightening and intense. You may say, "Oh no, he couldn't have meant that feeling. I can feel any other feeling, but not that one!" Yes, I do mean *that* feeling. If you're unable to experience or accept it, that's *precisely* the feeling that's going to cause you problems.

No one said this was going to be easy, but it is a solution. The life crippling addictions that we use to get rid of feelings do not work. If they did, we would not still have our addictions. We know our addictions don't work, we've tried them over and over and we're still unhappy, and still trying to find a way out of the trap. This is a way out. It's not an easy way out, it may not even be the only way out, but it is a way out.

Learn to understand your inner emotions, ideas, and beliefs. Learn to trust, care for, and accept yourself. And finally, learn to love yourself. Then *you* choose your life. This is possible and you can do it. As a psychologist, I see people change every day. I have faith in the ability of people to change and know they can learn to trust themselves and lead healthy, productive lives filled with quality and choice.

7

HEALTH

Stairs taken one step at a time.
A foot before the other I travel into tight aged rope
swinging in lifes' years, father time is with us
counting all our tears. Wooden shelf created to
gather all our dust. The clock our fathers crafted
seem to time me on this walk.
Every day reflections seem to age me with time.
The grey haired souls beside you only prove that
you have lost. A battle not worth fighting you must
accept the hourglass.
I search in life for knowledge and learn my days are
numbered. What kind of being would do this?
Measure us with life. I suppose the source of time
really has no matter. I must stop this clock from
ticking and free myself of this expiration date.

O ur own personal health is of obvious concern to all people. What is often *not* understood is how beliefs create our health or sickness. We are raised in a society that programs us into believing that health is something that is out of our personal control and that disease is thrust upon us. This is incorrect. This is a belief that is encouraged by society, by the medical profession, and by our own unwillingness to take responsibility for our health. This keeps us dependent on others for our personal well being. There is ample research, particularly in the last 20 years, that demonstrates that a person's ideas, beliefs, and willingness to take responsibility for their health are huge factors in maintaining and enhancing physical well-being.

Herbert Benson in his book *Timeless Healing* (1996) has fully reviewed the scientific research on the "placebo effect" and has reported that placebo therapy has a significant effect on a variety of medical complaints "the majority of the time." In other words, people who are given placebos, such as sugar pills, often benefit as much as individuals who are given a particular drug or medication. This is because they believe they are getting the drug or medication that is supposed to help their particular problem and their body then responds accordingly.

The research on hypnosis demonstrates that people's beliefs profoundly influence their physical body. For example, some highly suggestible hypnotic subjects who are told they are being touched with a red hot poker and are actually touched with a regular spoon, are able to raise blisters on their arm from the touching of the spoon. If your mind is able to alter your body in such a dramatic fashion through this concentrated belief, called hypnosis, think what you are able to do to your physical body through your daily, ongoing beliefs.

The catch here is that you are not only able to enhance your health through your beliefs but you are also able to destroy your health through your beliefs. While the medical and health professions are generally well-intended, some of what they do is harmful. One example is the warnings on cigarette packages: **"Surgeon General's Warning: Smoking Causes Lung Cancer, Heart Disease, Emphysema, And May Complicate Pregnancy."**

While it is true that people who regularly and excessively smoke affect their bodies in negative and unhealthy ways, it is also true that those who read the side of the cigarette package day after day, year after year, and then continue to smoke, affect their bodies in even more harmful ways. They are exposed to the constant, hypnotic suggestion that smoking is going to harm their health, and then they continue to do it anyway. They not only have the negative effects of the nicotine on their body, they also have the adverse body effects created by their belief in the dangers of smoking. When someone lights up a cigarette and says, "Here's one more nail in my coffin," this powerful, hypnotic suggestion will affect the body's response to the particular substance or chemical leading to more harm than if the person did not believe this to be so. I am *not* saying take the warnings off of cigarette packages. I am saying, be aware that your belief system affects the way chemicals and substances influence your body.

If you wake up every morning and tell yourself that a particular activity that you are doing is bad for your health, and then you continue to choose to do it, you will "reap what you sow" by inflicting negative self-messages, creating body responses based not only on your behavior, but also on your belief system. On the contrary, any particular activity that you believe is good for you is likely to be. For example, if you take vitamins every day and say to yourself, *and truly believe it,* "These vitamins are going to make me immune to disease", you are going to enhance any actual effect from the vitamins, and that very belief is going to improve your vitality and health. But, if you get up every morning and take your vitamins, telling yourself that you're only doing it because you were told to, and that in fact, vitamins have no effect on your health, then you are going to decrease any positive effect that the vitamins may have.

The Simonton's (1978) in Texas are known for their excellent cancer research. The Simonton's use an approach in which they utilize traditional medical treatments such as radiation and chemotherapy and add the use of hypnosis and imagery. Their patients are taught to visualize the chemotherapy and radiation attacking and destroying the cancer. They then help the patients to believe that this combats the cancer in a powerful way. This method utilizes the best of modern medicine and enhances it with our belief systems and mental abilities.

HEALTH HINTS

As an example of how to increase the power of traditional medicine, the next time you need to take an antibiotic for an infection, imagine it going to the infected area. Visualize the antibiotic attacking the infection, imagine yourself feeling healthier and healthier. Visualize yourself three or four days from then feeling good. Imagine yourself a month later being totally free of all disease. In other words, use the normal medical procedures that have been proven to be effective and enhance their effect with your own beliefs. Do not take an antibiotic and say to yourself "This isn't going to help me", or "They create more problems than they cure", because you are then decreasing any positive effect of the antibiotic. Even the name antibiotic which means anti-life, subliminally creates a negative view of the substance which decreases some of its usefulness.

Pay attention to what you say to yourself about your health. If you continually say, "I'm tired", "This is too much work", your body will respond accordingly and you will, in fact, be tired. Instead, if you notice that you feel tired, say to yourself "I'm going to sit down and I'm going to relax my entire body. I'm going to close my eyes. I'm going to slowly count from ten back to zero and with each number I will relax more and more completely. I'm going to allow myself ten minutes worth of total and complete rest, equal to several hours of good sleep." If you take that ten minute break and then tell yourself that you are refreshed, feeling good, and full of energy, you'll be amazed at the difference in how you feel.

If you are overweight and say to yourself "I'm fat and unhealthy", you are giving yourself a hypnotic suggestion on a daily basis that is very negative and will make it more difficult for you to lose weight no matter what diet you are on. Instead, enhance whatever you are doing to lose the weight by telling yourself that this particular technique or procedure is working and that you're feeling healthier everyday. Look in the mirror and see yourself as slimmer and trimmer. People will begin to respond to you as if you are slimmer and your body will begin to respond to these positive beliefs and suggestions that you and others are providing, and you will find yourself beginning to lose weight.

If you choose to sit down and eat a piece of cake while you're dieting, do not say to yourself "Every time I eat anything sweet, I put on another pound." If you do you will instruct your body to respond precisely the way that you don't want it to. If you're going to choose to eat something sweet, tell yourself that by eating only a small amount of it, you will feel completely satisfied and won't desire sweets again for a long time. And believe that eating that small amount of sweets is going to help you with your dieting because it is going to make you feel better about being on a diet.

Utilize these same suggestions in any area where you desire change. Use your beliefs to enhance your desired goal and do not self-talk the opposite of what you're attempting to accomplish.

AGING

As you begin to age, don't look at yourself and say, "Look how old I'm getting", rather say, "Look at the wisdom

I see in this face. Look at how I am softening and aging in a beautiful way." Instead of spending the day complaining about physical symptoms, enhance your health by thinking of aging as an opportunity to experience new adventures, meet new people, and to think of yourself in different ways.

Aging can be an opportunity to find value in yourself that isn't based on physical appearance or specific physical abilities. There are few things sadder than an 80-year-old person who has nothing to do except complain about the way they feel and talk about how unhappy they are. Life is to be lived, life is to be enjoyed, life is to be exciting. This requires that you stay in touch with your emotions, vitality, and joy. By reminding yourself that you are worthwhile and that life is enjoyable, you can wake up in the morning and say, "I'm glad to be alive today."

I have a patient who recently had her 50th birthday. This patient was a Hollywood hairdresser where she "rubbed elbows with the stars." She was also a longtime crack cocaine user with multiple family abuse issues. This created within her a belief that her only value was through her sexuality and her physical appearance. She spent her life attempting to gain approval from others through these attributes. And it worked as well as it could, given the superficial nature of this attempt to gain self-esteem.

However, for the last several years, this woman has increasingly been unable to maintain the facade of beauty, youth, and sexuality. As would be expected, the natural aging process and her harsh lifestyle has taken its toll. And now, she feels that she has no life and no value. She believes that no one could possibly want her, love her, or find her in any way useful or appealing.

This is because she has allowed her self-esteem to be totally based on youth, physical attractiveness, and sexuality. Now she is at a time in her life when she can no longer, even to herself, maintain this facade to gain illusory attention, approval, and love. While that attention, approval, and love may have been very superficial, it was all that this woman had for many years and now she feels that she has nothing. A very tragic and sad situation.

However, by "re-framing" her view of aging, and by learning that her self-esteem can be based on a different foundation, she is slowly beginning to realize that she has value apart from her sensuality and physical appearance. Rather than view aging as a loss of all that is worthwhile in her life, she is beginning to view aging as a flowering, a new growth, the other half of the book that is not yet written. She now sees it as an opportunity to obtain wisdom, and to share her life experiences with younger people. She is beginning to redeem some of the wreckage of her past through helping others so that they need not go to the extremes she has. This is simply a change of core belief. She is changing the core belief that all of her worth is dependent on her appearance, to a new belief that her worth has to do with other, more mature qualities.

PERSONAL RESPONSIBILITY

One area of psychological research called "internal" vs "external locus of control" (Rotter, 1954), demonstrates that people who think that they're responsible for their own health are healthier than people who think they're not. Those who score high on the external locus of control feel like disease "happens" to them. They believe that if they are around sick people, they will become ill. They believe there is nothing they can do to protect themselves from these external influences, and that once they are sick, the only way they can become healthy is to go to someone that prescribes something to eliminate this disease. It's as if it has nothing to do with them. Their body is some "object" that gets infected by dis-ease that then needs to be cured by some substance outside of themselves.

On the contrary, people who score high on internal locus of control, believe that they're responsible for their health. They believe it is up to them to keep their immune system functioning at a high level and they believe they can be around sick people without getting sick. Or, if they do become ill, they believe there are things they can do to help themselves get well. These people basically see themselves as responsible for their own good health. They are much healthier than people who believe they are not responsible for their health.

The message is that your body responds the way that you believe. If you believe that you can influence your body, and be responsible for the health of your body, then that will be so. But if you believe that you are a victim of disease, then that will be so.

Every day in the media there's news of some new cancer producing substance. Some other food item that should not be eaten. We *have* to eat something, and if we continue to eat these "cancer producing" foods believing we're going to get sick, our body will respond accordingly. The alternative here is to recognize that we have a natural, built-in immune system that keeps us free from dis-ease.

Think of your immune system as being *powerful,* believe you are healthy. Recognize you have a *powerful immune system* that protects you from the influence of minor chemicals in the environment, and promotes your daily good health. Take responsibility for your health, no one else is going to do it for you.

As a psychologist, I've had many patients in hospital settings and consequently had the opportunity to work regularly with nurses and medical doctors. Generally speaking, I believe the great majority of health care providers are extremely well intended and have devoted their lives to helping people. However, they are often some of the least healthy people I have met. What I suggest is, that if you are going to allow others besides yourself to be in charge of your personal health, find others that are healthy themselves.

There are certainly times in life when we need help from others. I am not saying that we can do it all, all the time, for ourselves. I am saying that if you are going to look to others for help, look to others that represent the ideal that you are trying to obtain. Look to those who have learned how to create and maintain a high level of emotional and physical well being in their own life. If you want to learn about parenting, go to good parents; if you want to learn about emotional health, go to emotionally healthy people. If you want to learn about physical health, go to physically healthy people. These are the people that have found ways to heal themselves. These are the ones that have learned how to utilize their beliefs in the most complimentary way.

8

PERSONAL FINANCE AND BUSINESS

Do you think it's all for free
Where'd you get your wealth
Well it wasn't just given to me
Life's a long path and nothing is for free
We're living in a world of money and greed
So hard I've tried to make ends meet, almost
gave up, thought I was beat, till that day when
the rubber met the street
Financial troubles are a bitch but you meet your
problems inch by inch
Little patience, little time, but life works it out to a fine line

What you believe about yourself and your capabilities will influence how you act in the business world. When you believe you are capable and you are determined to be successful, you will be. Conversely, if you believe you are inadequate and incapable and approach business with a lack of confidence, you will be unsuccessful. If you believe that to be successful you have to cut every corner and cheat everybody possible, even if you're successful, you will be guarded, paranoid, unhappy, and constantly vigilant. But, if you believe that good things come your way, without undue stress or anxiety, you are likely to be successful in a comfortable and pleasurable way.

Beliefs, like in all other areas of life, create our personal finances. There are segments of society that believe they are trapped into poverty, and by believing so they continue the spiral of poverty. There are other people who are born into monied families, where money is taken for granted. While they may have money, they may not appreciate the value of it, or how others have worked to obtain professional or financial success.

In the business world, how you carry yourself and how you feel about yourself is going to be apparent to all those around you including your supervisors. Those people who appear confident, competent, and motivated, exude confidence to others and find themselves obtaining rewards in their professional and financial lives.

If you find yourself pleased with your financial and business endeavors, then continue to promote those beliefs that are creating success. Be aware of the good feelings, ideas, thoughts, and beliefs that you have about your abilities.

Expand on them, concentrate on them. Remind yourself daily of your personal and business habits that are encouraging success. Feel good about this success and good about your abilities.

If, on the other hand, you find yourself feeling unsuccessful, always stressed over money, believing that no matter how hard you try, financial success is hopeless, then you need to closely examine the limiting beliefs leading to these ideas and feelings. You will find that underneath these feelings and behaviors, core beliefs are creating them. These core beliefs are likely connected to your ideas about money, success, or very personal ideas about yourself.

For example, if you have been born into a family or culture that believes that "money is the root of all evil" and that people who have money are less spiritual than those without money, you will avoid financial success in order to be spiritual. On the other hand, if you feel that God's bounty is here on earth and that financial success should be a natural part of your spiritual success, you will create those changes and decisions that bring financial wealth to you.

In the 1960s, there was a generation of "hippies" that stressed ideals which were generally opposed to upper middle-class thinking. They had often been raised by parents who seemed obsessed with materialism and their philosophy was that those things just don't matter. To some extent, that was a good swing for the pendulum to take. Focusing on peace, love, and the environment was certainly a needed positive emphasis. But, rejecting the natural benefits of hard work and ambition did not create spirituality, only poverty. There is no reason that you can't emphasize ecological, moral, and spiritual values *and* enjoy financial success. These are not incompatible unless you believe them to be.

Many business people who stress financial gain only, believe they have to lose their morality, put their ethics aside, and lose concern about other's welfare in order to compete in the "game" of business and finance. This is not true. You can emphasize business and financial success without it interfering with your emotional, ethical, or spiritual life.

These limiting ideas come, as always, from core beliefs that have remained unexamined. If you wish to be successful in finance or business, start by making a list of your beliefs about financial success. Write down the beliefs you have about your business and financial abilities. The reasons why you believe you are going to succeed or not. The reasons why you feel that you haven't yet been successful. Note which beliefs are useful and promote success and which are like personal hypnotic suggestions that promote failure.

Business and financial success are not good or bad by themselves. They are simply another opportunity, or choice, that we can have in our life. To throw away our humanity in order to obtain financial success is unnecessary and damaging. On the other hand, to limit our success because of misguided ideas about what it means to be "spiritual" or "moral" is also unnecessary and limits our legitimate life choices.

There is an excellent, readable book called *The Richest Man in Babylon* (Clason, 1926), that concisely offers some basic principles of financial gain and stability which, by their very nature, begin to correct limiting beliefs that many of us hold regarding finances. In the book's words the primary simple rules of acquisition are:

1) "Start thy purse to fattening"
2) "Control thy expenditures"
3) "Make thy gold multiply"
4) "Guard thy treasures from loss"
5) "Make of thy dwelling a profitable investment"
6) "Insure a future income"
7) "Increase thy ability to earn"

Thinking about these simple and ancient rules, from the standpoint of Belief Therapy, it becomes clear that there are certain principles or beliefs which will bring about prosperity in the same way that certain beliefs bring about good health or success in other areas.

In this book it is stated that "I found the road to wealth when I decided that a part of all I earn was mine to keep and so will you." Believing that a part of all that you earn is truly yours to keep, allows you then to put aside some portion of all of your earnings. By putting aside some portion of all of your earnings, you begin to find that you start to accrue capital. It is clear that in order to gain any kind of wealth, you first have to begin to obtain it. It is only by believing that you have a right to some portion of everything that you earn that you begin to accrue wealth. Once you truly believe and act on this basic principle, you begin to put aside a portion of your earnings.

For example, those of you who have been working for 15, 20, 30, or even 40 years, and you look in your bank account now and realize that you have no funds. Ask yourself, "What if I'd only taken ten cents out of every dollar that I ever earned and put it in the bank?" Even if it were only earning two or three percent in that account, what would it be today? People often think; "It's too late to start now" or "I need every penny that I earn in order to pay my debts." Is it too late? Do you need it all? Think about it. If suddenly you were forced to live on 90 percent of your income, would you survive? Of course you would. You would just do with a little bit less. You would do with ten percent less. And if that ten percent had been accruing with a normal rate of interest through the years you'd been in the work force, consider the investment you would have. This is how to accrue income. This demonstrates principle number one: "Start thy purse to fattening."

Number two: "Control thy expenditures." This is pretty straight forward. One way to make sure you have ten percent of your income to always put away, is to control how much you spend. I'm not talking huge amounts. I'm not saying, "Don't buy the children new shoes" or, "Eat beans and rice for dinner." I am saying, slice out one small portion of your income, put it away, and forget it. And by controlling your expenditures, you'll find that easy to do.

The third principle is: "Make thy gold multiply." In this society the easiest and safest way to do that is through interest. Interest, while it appears small, multiplies. When you begin to accrue income at an interest rate in a totally safe investment, your principal over a ten, 15, or 20 year period, creates dramatic savings. And it provides you with financial security.

Rule number four: "Guard thy treasures from loss." There is nothing worse than working hard, saving your money, and then losing it and having to do it all over again. Many of us have had that experience. So, when you consider investments, a basic rule is to guard the principle. If you never lose the percentage saved and it continues to accrue, day after day, month after month, year after year, then you will always have a solid foundation of wealth. If you decide to "play with the money" and invest in areas that require more risk and more potential profit, do it with the interest, not with the principle.

Rule number five: "Make of thy dwelling a profitable investment." In other words live in your own house. It has the advantage of tax write-offs and equity improvement over time. Real estate currently is not the growing market that it was, but it is still a safe, sound, secure investment, particularly for the individual home owner.

Rule number six: "Insure a future income." This is most easily done by having some portion of your principle in "safe" investments that will not deteriorate.

Rule number seven: "Increase thy ability to earn." In other words, believe in yourself and believe in your ability to accrue wealth. Believe in your skills, and rather than figuring out how to avoid work, figure out how to enjoy it. Make work a pleasure. Look forward to your activities that produce income. Look at your beliefs in regard to work. Do you see work as something negative and to be avoided? Do you see it as belittling?

Find activities that produce income and provide you with pleasure and pride in your workmanship. Find a career where you wake up in the morning and do not dread going to work that day. This is essential for the long-term ability to increase your earning potential. If you enjoy work and it has meaning for you, you will do a good job. If you do a good job, your ability to earn will continue to improve.

Following these seven simple suggestions and closely examining your beliefs that limit your ability to earn will allow you to begin to obtain the personal wealth you so desire. Look at how your beliefs impact and affect your work performance. Write down your beliefs about your current occupation and then write down your beliefs, ideas, and dreams about what you would like to be doing in five years. See if what you are doing today is leading you towards where you want to be. And if it is not, consider why not. Examine the obstacles. If you continue doing exactly what you are doing today, where will you be in five years? How does that compare with the vision you have of where you want to be? By looking towards the future, as well as looking closely at the present, you can mold the present to create the financial future that you want.

9

VIOLENCE IN AMERICA

Distant screams can you hear them?
The smell of death as you get near them.
The rise of steam leaks from the dying,
beside the dead mothers crying
Pools of blood and scattered bodies,
the freezing air of this misty morning
A loss of lives that can never be replaced,
when left up to our nature you find the
extinction of our race.

Of grave concern to all people, particularly in our society, is the rampant violence that we see on the streets today. This violence appears to be growing daily with no end in sight. Of enormous concern is the degree of violence among our youth. It can be argued that we have always been a violent culture and there is some truth to that. However, now there seems to be runaway violence, much of which is not even goal directed. In the past, when a store was robbed, typically the money was taken and the proprietors were left alone. Currently more often, when people commit a crime of greed, they also commit a crime of violence. It is more and more common to see people enter a convenience store, take what cash they can, and then shoot the employee or owner before leaving. This is alarming and it indicates core beliefs that are destructive for our culture and ourselves. It suggests beliefs that lack awareness of the sanctity of life. It is as if these people see no value in life; either their own or others.

When you look at the eyes of the gang members that have been on the streets too long, you see no life. They are already dead. They have so suppressed their humanity and emotions, that they no longer have compassion or empathy for anyone. This allows them to take great risks and to kill with no compunction, and to be killed with little fear.

These youths have so denied their feelings that they truly care about nothing. In order to feel a spark of life, it is necessary for them to experience intense, powerful, environmental excitement. This is the reason why they are attracted to drive-by shootings, drugs, violence, and living on the edge. When people suppress their emotions for too long, they are forced to live in a narrow band of sensation. This produces a chronic emptiness or boredom and a feeling of "Is

93

this all there is?" To break out of this straight-jacket of deadness, it is often necessary for them to be involved in intense life-threatening activities in order to feel alive. Unfortunately, these activities often lead to more repressed feelings, narrowing down this "band of sensation" even further, which then creates a need to seek more excitement and danger in order to break through the life-constricting repression. This spiraling system leads to increased repression, constriction, deadness, and eventual acting out behaviors.

Once again, the core problem is that we have not been taught in this culture to deal with our feelings. We have been taught to avoid and suppress our feelings, distrust others and ourselves, and to reach for a chemical or a substance as a magic answer to "get rid of" these unwanted feelings. We are a culture that believes in a magic answer: If we don't like what we're feeling, we must get rid of it now. But in our attempt to deaden ourselves, we create violence not only towards others, but emotionally toward ourselves.

What are some of the factors that contribute to the violence and the deadening in our children? One of the problems we see today is children growing up in families without reasonable guidelines. Children growing up believing there are no limits to their behavior. And often when they have one or both parents working long hours, it is difficult for these parents to set appropriate guidelines. Many times there are no limits enforced because there is no one present to enforce them. Or if there is, they are so overwhelmed with their own issues and life difficulties they don't have the necessary energy to parent their children appropriately.

Children raised without guidelines or supervision "act out" behaviors, which trigger powerful emotions that are frightening to the child. The child then looks for help in understanding and appropriately expressing these emotions. However, there is no one there to help. This leaves the child on their own with no recourse but to begin the process of repression and denial, which eventually leads to emotional constriction and more "acting out" behaviors to release the pressure in the "pressure cooker", continuing the destructive spiral towards violence and deadness in our youth.

As the child grows they become even more sophisticated in their attempts to suppress feelings, often using drugs, alcohol, and other destructive defenses. This efficiency in deadening themselves leads to new and more extreme forms of "acting out" to release the tension and to create temporary feelings of aliveness.

Without learning appropriate ways of dealing with their feelings through parental modeling and guidance, our children are doomed to repeat this cycle. As adults they then help create the phenomenon of rampant violence so apparent today.

Related to this issue is what has become known as "children's rights." In the 1960's, a useful movement towards respecting and acknowledging children's rights began. However, like many other issues, it's possible for the "pendulum" to swing too far. We currently live in a culture where parents are held fully responsible for their teenager's behavior but have very few options as to how to control that same behavior. Children are clearly taught today (and rightly so), where to go or who to talk to if they feel that they are being verbally, physically, or emotionally abused. However, parental behavior has become so scrutinized by legal agencies, teachers, neighbors, and well-meaning friends, that parents often feel impotent to control their child's behavior without being accused of some type of abuse.

If your teenager stands up and says, "I'm leaving" and you say, "You can't go", and he says "I'm going anyway, what are you going to do about it?", and you place your hands on him in an attempt to stop him, you may be accused of child abuse. On the other hand, if you don't stop him and he leaves and commits a crime, you will be held responsible for his or her behavior. Charges may be filed due to your inability to stop him or her from committing the crime.

Parents today are often "between a rock and a hard place." One of the unfortunate results of this situation is that it allows children to do whatever they want while parents feel helpless, hopeless, and fearful.

Small children naturally feel omnipotent and all-powerful. It is through the parent's loving guidance, structure, and control that this sense of omnipotence is typically curbed at a young age. However, with the current political climate, we are raising a generation of children who no longer believe that there are limits and guidelines they need follow. They have continued this sense of omnipotence far past the natural age that it should have been stopped. These children have not learned to control their impulses or behavior. They have not learned how to express their emotions, or to trust and accept their feelings. Consequently, their emotions run away into inappropriate acting out behaviors, and they eventually hurt either themselves or others.

These children have not learned to respect guidelines; they have not learned to respect their parents; and, therefore, they have not learned to respect themselves. They are empty inside with only anxiety, meaninglessness, and purposeless, often violent, behavior to keep them company.

The solutions to deep problems of this type are not to be found in outward restraints. Additional laws and longer prison sentences will *not* solve the violence in America. If it could, it would have already. We must look more closely at the early beliefs that our children are being taught. We must examine our own attitudes and ideas and learn to deal with our own emotions in appropriate ways.

If we cannot come to terms with our limiting beliefs and repressed emotions, how can we teach our children any better. We are failing as a society to teach our children self-restraint, self-respect, self-trust, or self-love. And, if they do not have these attributes for themselves, they *will not* have them for others. Behavioral restraint ultimately comes from a strong sense of self-identity and self-care. Our focus as a society needs to be in teaching *values* first; at home, in school, *and* in the media. Without proper priorities these difficult problems are likely to continue and even increase in the years to come.

10

RELIGION AND SPIRITUALITY

Between the grip of ones love
is mother wing with songs above.
Where do angels sometimes go?
Loss of hope the winter snow.
My eyes they wander,
want to stand beneath the midnight sky.
Please don't fail to understand
in my mind fate tells no lie.
And I shall never say goodbye
only spread my wings and fly.

We live in a world where Protestants and Catholics are killing each other over their beliefs about God. A world where Moslems kill Hindus, Christians kill Moslems, Jews, and Moslems kill each other, over their beliefs about God. A world where peaceful people have been invaded and forced to adopt the prevailing religious views of the invaders, all in the name of God. We live in a society where we are often taught that God is judgmental, God is harsh, God is all-powerful, and God is watching us. That if we do not behave in certain specific ways, designated by our religious leaders, parents, teachers, or the prevailing religious views of our culture, we will be punished. Not only will we be punished, we may well be punished eternally, forever and ever, likely in a world of fire and brimstone, pain and cruelty, all for not having been willing and able to live up to the expectations of this harsh and judgmental God.

We live in a world where we are taught that there is an opposing force called the Devil, or Satan, who is against God and is able to influence us and force us into bad behaviors. Possibly a force powerful enough to capture our immortal soul forever and take us into a place of darkness, pain, and suffering. We are often told to give up our will to God, and then we are told that Satan can take over our will. In this context, we are told that we should not have free will, and that we should use our will to follow God's will.

Who is this God that we are supposed to give our will over to and trust in his better judgment? A judgmental God that tells us we will be punished, we're bad, we're sinful, and undeserving. Are we to prostrate ourselves before this God, beg for his mercy for having been so bad? Sexuality, competition, self love, envy, jealousy, a lack of devotion to God, many of these "transgressions" are apparently sufficient to doom us to an eternity of pain, darkness, and hell. For what? For not having sufficient respect, devotion, and adoration for this angry, judgmental, vengeful God that sees fit to destroy people who don't follow his rules? If this is what God is all about, then I want no part of him.

How confusing as a child to be brought up in a culture that on the one hand teaches you to fear God and on the other hand talks of God's love and mercy. How confusing to be told to exercise your free will and your discipline to do good things, but then, to be told that there's a powerful Satanic force, apparently almost as powerful as the all-powerful God, that can influence you and force you to do bad things. How confusing to believe that your very thoughts, ideas, fantasies, and dreams are somehow exposed to this all-powerful, vengeful, judgmental God. And, that if these inner fantasies are not "acceptable" you may be punished unmercifully. Children are taught to be non-judgmental, taught not to be racially biased or sexually biased, then are told that "Godless" people that don't believe in a particular religion or belief are going to be judged by God and sent to hell for eternity. Often our children are exposed to daily news where "Godly" people are busily killing each other in the name of their different Gods. With each side or religion believing "God" is on *their* side and that the enemy are godless heathens.

Religion, as it is generally taught today, strikes at the very heart of the concept of free will. It is often contradictory to self-esteem, self-respect, and self-care. Children watch televangelists preach about God on Sunday morning and then they read the evening newspaper and learn that the same evangelist that was preaching so hard and so long has just been arrested on charges of catering to prostitutes, money fraud, or some other "sin" he was preaching against earlier that day.

If beings from another planet landed here today, with no particular biases, and examined the world of organized religion, they would conclude that we're all mad. And yet, this is the climate in which we raise our children, and this is the climate that creates powerful, conflicting core beliefs about the nature of good and evil, justice and injustice, heaven and hell.

How frightening to be a small child, at the mercy of large, powerful parental figures, and also at the mercy of this unknown, judgmental God. How frightening for a child to believe that their natural feelings of excitement, exuberance, and playfulness, are consistently watched and judged. How frightening to believe that he or she may be punished at any time, possibly forever, for those same feelings, thoughts, ideas, and dreams that are natural to every child.

How many of us today carry around harsh, self-critical judgments of a multitude of natural behaviors because we were taught as children to think of them as sinful? How many of us have difficulty in normal sexuality because we believe we are doing something bad in God's eyes? How many of us judge our sexual thoughts and dreams and wonder if we may somehow be punished for them.

Often we spend our whole life trying to live up to some impossible standard of goodness and holiness set by parents or religious leaders, only to find, at the end of it all, we look back and say, "Is that all there was?" We realize how much life we've lost through this pursuit of a standard to which no human being should be or could be expected to live up to and no truly loving God would expect.

Where do these ideas come from? Up until the advent of modern technology, religion had many different ideas about God figures. For example, many God figures were considered to be female. There was the mother earth, the moon goddess, the loving goddess, the goddess of fertility, and so on. There were certainly as many female goddesses as there were male gods. And the female side, the non-violent, receptive, life-giving side, was considered to be all a part of the Godhead.

Why should God be male? We take this concept for granted in this culture, and yet in the history of "mankind", God has not always been male or even predominantly male. Pick up any book and you find that most sentences say, "He did." You don't often see, "She did."

Why is that? Because maleness in this culture has been idolized to justify conquest. How useful is that concept any longer? Why shouldn't the Godhead be female? It is the female that carries and bears life.

As technology progressed, we moved towards the belief that it was our duty, our *"God-given duty"* to *conquer* the earth, rather than to live in harmony with the earth. The male God became prominent over the female Goddess and was typically portrayed as angry, vengeful, and judgmental. This god was presented as a God of aggression and conquest. Following this model, we have been busy conquering the earth and each other ever since. We cannot live on a planet that we have ravished and destroyed in order to prove that we own it. Tribal cultures have always known this fact but we seem to have forgotten it. When Columbus discovered the new world there were thousands of American natives living here. How do you "discover" a continent that has been inhabited since the beginning of time? And, after you discover this continent, "in God's name", what gives you the "God-given" right to conquer these people and call it your own?

We have a history of conquest and exploitation. We conquer each other, we conquer the animals, the plants, the sea, and the sky. Now we can't drink the water or breathe the air, and even the land is becoming uninhabitable.

The problem is that we are all sharing a huge, core belief that says *"God is on our side"* and that belief justifies *anything* we do to each other or the world around us. That belief has to be changed. God is not vengeful. God is not violent. God does not want us to conquer other peoples. God does not want us to conquer the planet and God is *not* on our side when we do so. Until we see this clearly, we will continue to threaten all life.

I believe that God is not looking over us, judging us, and requiring us to conquer and exploit. That is simply a belief about reality that we have been taught, and that our parents were taught, and their parents were taught. God does not demand that we convert other people to our way of thinking. God does not demand that we take over other countries just because they don't think like us. God does not demand that we take over the planet and destroy the natural ecological balance of millions of years. We need to rethink both our beliefs and our behavior!

Let's consider the possibility that spirituality, *not reli - gion, but spirituality,* is neither male nor female, that it is perhaps a creative, loving, organizing, energetic influence. To think in those terms, one is left with a single conclusion: People have free will, they exercise their free will, and they are responsible for their free will. With this belief, we no longer need Satan to oppose us. We no longer need a god to set models and ideals for us to follow. We need only to take responsibility for ourselves... responsibility for our free will, our behavior, actions, and emotions, as well as care and love for ourselves. When we do this, our behavior takes on a natural pattern where we allow people to think the way they think, we allow the natural balance on the planet to continue, and we allow ourselves to live in harmony with ourselves and with others.

This huge, collective core belief in a vengeful, angry God that wants everyone to think like him, puts a burden on every person that holds this belief. It's incorrect. *It is wrong.* It was useful at a time when our society needed to be thrusting out and expanding, and we needed to be fighting against ourselves in order to develop a technology to control and to use the earth's resources. *We have done that.* We are now over-balanced, we no longer need to learn how to control and use the planet's resources. In fact, we are about to run out of the planet's resources. We now need to adopt a loving technology where we live in harmony with each other. We cannot do that with a concept of God as being warlike and proselytizing. This will not continue to work.

I suggest that each of us take time to write down our beliefs about God, religion, and spirituality. Write down all the confusing, contradictory ideas that you were taught as a child: "God is loving"; "God is merciful"; "God is angry"; "God is vengeful"; "God demands that you convert your neighbor to your beliefs." Realize the contradictory nature of these beliefs. Realize the destructive nature of any belief system that says, "God is on my side and it is my duty to convert other people to my way of thinking." These other people are not going to allow us to convert them to our way of thinking.

We have ample history to show that trying to convert other people to our way of thinking destroys their culture, kills people, and destroys the natural ecological balance and harmony. It is essential that *all of us* begin to examine our religious views, both past and current, and consider the usefulness of them in our present day, modern world.

Who do you want God to be? Do you want God to be a vengeful God or do you want God to be a caring, loving God? Is it necessary to you that God be male? Do you *real - ly* think there's some being up there sitting on a cloud with a long white beard, writing down everything we do, waiting to judge us at the end of our lives? Or, is that more like a fairy tale that was useful at some time in our past but has outlived its usefulness?

I believe it's time we outgrew these immature and non-useful concepts of God, and I believe that if we don't out-grow them, they will destroy us. I believe that continuing to idolize leaders, political or religious, that believe these concepts of God is a serious mistake. Why not stop that and begin instead to look for leaders who embody a loving technology, a loving spirituality, and a loving harmony between people everywhere?

Ultimately, *this* comes down to these things: Examining our long-held core beliefs, looking at them clearly in today's aware-consciousness from a standpoint of freedom, free will and free choice, and deciding how we wish to think and what is the most useful way to proceed. This would change our lives dramatically. Instead of feel-ing like a sinner, and that you have to *earn* your way to God, you would feel that freedom and joy are your birthrights, freely given to all.

Perhaps, "original sin" was just a necessary belief to control people, and it is no longer needed. Perhaps, now what we need is personal responsibility to control ourselves. Perhaps, now what we need is a philosophy that embodies free will. It's time that each of us assume responsibility for ourselves. In order to do that, we have to realize we are *free* and that we do have free will. No one, not Satan and not God, is up there, or down there, pulling strings and manipulating our behavior. Therefore, we have to pull our own strings and be responsible for our own lives. These old, immature ideas about religion and God must be very, very confusing to children because they're certainly confusing to adults. And one of the reasons they're confusing is because they're built on archaic, core beliefs that may well have been useful then, but are no longer useful now.

It's interesting that many of us are taught to believe that whenever we do something wrong, it's our fault, but whenever we do something right, it's because it was God's will. When do we get to feel good about ourselves? At what point do we get to take credit for our behavior? If we are going to be blamed for the wrongs we do, then let's at least give ourselves credit for the rights that we do.

How about a whole new idea? Let's take responsibility for *all* of our behavior, believing that we have free will, and, therefore, *our behaviors are our responsibility.* Then, when a particular behavior is performed, we don't have to look for someone to blame or someone to give credit to. When we blame Satan or we give credit to God, we cripple ourselves and we take away our ability to act because we do not see that we are responsible.

Think about the word "responsible." Response-able, able to respond. As long as we believe that it is God's will, acting through us, or Satan's will, forcing us to do something, we continue not to be response-able. In other words, we are *irresponsible.* And that's precisely how too many of us continue to act. We continue to behave in irresponsible, not responsible ways. It's time to closely examine these old, limiting, non-useful beliefs and learn to be response-able.

I would like to take this opportunity to add to the confusion by sharing my personal philosophy. I believe that

God is an impersonal God, an incredibly wonderful, creative, life-giving, organizing, energetic principle that offers
freedom and free will to each of his or her creatures. Free
will, free choice and with that, the responsibility that
always comes with choice. Because if we're not being influenced, then we are responsible for our decisions and our
choices. If we all were willing to take responsibility for
whatever choices and freedoms that we utilized, I believe
the earth would be a different and better place.

So, in my beliefs about God, God is neither male nor
female. God does not watch over me and give me advice or
punish me for wrong doings. I *have* to believe that God
allows and promotes free will and choice. Without it, we're
all robots, either being influenced by Satan or influenced
by God. A loving God would not prohibit us from having
choices and being responsible for our own lives.

I see no reason to believe in Satan. If you accept the
idea of free will and personal responsibility, you really
don't need to go further because all the evils and joys of
the world can be explained by free will. We can choose to
be loving, we can choose to be considerate, we can choose
to deal with our problems and emotions and to have a life
of quality. Or, we can choose to run from ourselves and
run from others. We can choose to believe that we are
more special and important than others and that God's on
our side. In so believing, we can take other's freedoms
away even to the extreme of death. We can choose to
believe that other people have no value and that we're the
only ones that have any rights. We can strip the rights of
others through violence and victimization. *Free will is
enough to explain everything!* We don't need a Satanic force
trying to influence people, we don't even need a benevolent
force trying to influence us for the good.

This view may not be as comforting as believing in a
personal God that's watching over you, but it has the
advantage of making us responsible for ourselves and
our world. We can't blame God for not giving us the
"answer", we can't blame the devil for misleading us. If
we do something good, uplifting, or altruistic, *we* get the

credit for it, not God. If we do something that is limiting, shallow, and destructive, *we* get the credit for that too, not Satan. Therefore, we are responsible for our choices, whether they are good or bad, destructive or life-giving.

My core beliefs lean towards a universe of personal freedom and responsibility. I think our particular planet, and galaxy and universe, are like grains of sand on all the planets, on all the galaxies, in all the "beaches", of all the universes. I believe space and time goes forwards and backwards, in and out, up and down. I think we are all children, with budding intellects, barely beginning to comprehend the smallest idea of "what it's all about" and then only dimly. I often think we are like kindergartners trying to understand trigonometry and nuclear physics and then wondering why we can't get it. I don't think we are ready yet to "get it" with our limited intellect and technology. I think "its" more something that needs to be "sensed" at an intuitive level.

I believe it's a mistake to think that our intellect is all that we are. If true, that's frightening, because to date our intellect has not done a very good job of promoting life on this planet. The dinosaurs were around for millions of years longer than we have been, and we're *already* creating ecological problems of immense proportions. It's hard to imagine us making it even a fraction of the time of the dinosaurs if we don't change.

11

DEATH AND DYING

Flowers of grief grown before me
Planted in my past
The endless tears that cease to last
Petals I see them dying and I know I'm fading fast
The flower of grief, my warning
of a future broken glass
This dead black rose it's growing
into a realm of which won't last
So save me Mother Mourning
Lead me from earth's graveyard grass

We all die. And we have a multitude of philosophies for explaining the death experience and/or the life-after-death experience. Most rational people would say, "Who really knows anyway?" We still haven't had many folks coming back after death explaining their experience to us. At least not in any verifiable way that we can put on the Channel 5 news. So, we know we die, and unless you believe that one small group of people have the truth and everyone else is wrong, we generally assume that we don't know what happens after death.

No matter which philosophy or core belief you adopt, death is a reality in your life and in the lives around you. Even if you believe that your loved ones are going up to heaven to wait for you, and will be exactly as they were when they left, when you lose someone you love, they're *gone now*! They are no longer here with you today. And, experiencing the despair, grief and pain that this creates is absolutely essential to heal the loss. Trying to deny the pain by saying, "Oh well, they're in heaven and they're in a better place", *does not work*. Even if true, you're here and they're not here with you. The fact that you've lost someone you love, and that you can no longer be with them, is something to grieve about. And it's something that we're absolutely helpless to change.

We may have ample freedom to change and control ourselves, but we have zero degree of freedom to control others. By the very nature of free will, others ultimately are not controllable. This means that to be alive and aware, you have to risk and you have to get hurt. That's part of the deal. There is no way around that. As long as you're here, why not be alive? And if you're alive, it means you have to be open to your emotions. If you are, that means you are going to suffer losses. You can deny those losses and try to get rid of them with drugs, alcohol, or other obsessive and addictive behaviors, or you can accept them and accept that these feelings are a part of life. It's my choice to accept the losses in my life and feel the feelings connected with them. By doing so I allow healing to take place and free myself to be fully aware and alive.

If I deny the unavoidable pain in life and close my heart, then I've killed myself a little bit. The more that happens, the more I deaden and numb my pain. Eventually I might as well be dead myself, because I'm alive, yet no longer *alive*. I am not in touch with the feelings that make us human, the intimacy and the love that makes life worth living.

Whatever your core beliefs about death and dying, I suggest that when faced with that kind of loss, you allow yourself to feel. The grief is like waves coming in from the ocean. One wave comes in and it's a little steep, cold and frightening and then after that, maybe it's a smaller wave, and then there's no wave for a little while, and then here comes another one. There is a natural rhythm to the waves and the grief, and there's a natural biological healing that is taking place.

RITUALS

In most cultures, throughout time, there are methods to accept loss. Some cultures would cut out a big chunk of their hair. In Indian cultures the hair was long, it would take over a year to grow back and every day the griever was reminded of their loss. In other cultures, after a major loss, women wore black for a year. This reminded them and others that they were grieving and that it was okay to take the necessary time to heal. In this culture, we have forgotten these natural ways of wisdom. When someone we love dies, we seem to believe that a week later, a month later, or six months later, it's supposed to be all over. It's time to be out there dating again and enjoying life. We hear things like, "It's okay, they are in a better place", or "It's time you started getting on with your life."

No, it's not time that you "get on with your life" until it's time. Only your body knows its own rhythm of grief. Your mind can say, "Oh, I should be over this now", but your body knows whether or not you are. The grief and the emotions locked in the body need to be expressed. You need to give yourself permission to talk to others, cry, be angry; whatever it takes and however *long* it takes. That is the natural healing process. Be gentle with yourself because you are alive. Life, at times, is painful, but it is all we have.

Don't let others be the guide for your emotions, pay attention to your dreams, pay attention to your feelings, pay attention to your body. Pay attention to the natural rhythms within you, the natural healing, the natural flow, the natural movement. Learn to respect yourself and to trust yourself. You are your own best parent. And if you examine your ideas and beliefs honestly and learn to accept and trust your emotions fully, you will feel fully alive and able to experience all that life has to offer. The sunsets and flowers, the love and pain, the heartbreak and joy; that is all part of life. What more could we ask for when we are alive, but to live. When I am gone, what I want them to say about me is, "While he was here, he was truly alive."

12

THE ENVIRONMENT

Cried in black mourning for a death you still must feel
Sang with the angels that alter your fear
Walked with the reaper he spoke of you there
Danced with the devil and now you must beware
I searched your four senses,
Summer, Spring, Winter & Fall
Your summers are ash and in spring the grounds are dead
In winter ice it kills the chance for anything to live
Fall it captures pictures of something you have killed
The Earth

We have cultural core beliefs that are causing us to treat our earth as if it were an object, rather than a living being upon which our very survival depends. For many reasons (technology, money, power, control), both good and bad, we have learned to extract ourselves from our environment. We have learned to think of ourselves as different from the trees and the animals, the waters and the mountains. When we think of ourselves as different, we also think of ourselves as more important. We believe we have the right to do whatever we want, whenever we want, just because we are able. We believe that because we have developed the necessary technology, that we must use it to manipulate, destroy, and conquer. This is a short-sided view. Another short-term solution to a long-term problem. It may create an initial degree of comfort for some of us, but it is destroying the very place upon which we have to survive. This is not a solution, it is destruction. We *cannot* continue the way we have.

Some of our lack of respect for our environment comes from the belief that we are going to die anyway, so what do we care about the future? We *are* more than separate, conscious identities. We *are* connected to all life in ways that we can only begin to imagine. And, we *do* have a responsibility to our children, our grandchildren, our great-grandchildren, and to the other life forms with which we share the planet. If we're going to develop technology with the capability of destroying life, then we must develop the morality and responsibility that goes with that technology.

To date, it appears that we have adopted technology without morality. We are biological, the trees are biological, the earth is biological, the animals are biological. We are connected at that level, and if we are

119

the ones capable of destroying all of this, then we have to be the ones responsible enough *not* to. To think only of ourselves and not care what happens after our death is based on a core belief of separateness, individuality, and a belief that there is nothing else. That's a very limiting belief.

Most tribal cultures think of themselves as being connected with the earth, moon, sun, and all life. They think of themselves as being greater than their individual identity and they attempt to live in harmony with their surroundings. Recognizing that while they may die tomorrow, they still remain as part of the overall balance of life. Over-identifying with our individual ego and believing that's all there is, and all that's important, encourages irresponsible and destructive acts towards ourselves, and all life.

A life *promoting* belief, that would encourage us to change this behavior, would be to consider ourselves a part of *All That Is*. A part of the trees, a part of the waters, a part of the sky, and a part of each other. Not in some impersonal "nirvana" where we have no individual consciousness and are swallowed like a "drop in the sea", but rather a conscious, intelligent, aware appreciation of the interdependence of all living things. We *are* a part of *All That Is*, whether we accept it or not, whether we believe it or not, or whether we act like it or not. We are made of the same substances. To one degree or another, we all share consciousness. We certainly have a very defined and discreet individual consciousness, which we call "you and I" or "me and you", but we also have a global awareness and underlying, biological connectedness to all life. That connectedness requires morality and responsibility for other living beings. If we are going to be the technological giants on this planet, then we must also be responsible for that technology and make it a loving, caring technology, not an exploitive, destructive one.

Seeing the truth of our interconnectedness and interdependence with all life, would create a loving technology aimed towards promoting life, not towards destroying it. We can learn to live together on this planet in harmony. To many that sounds like the greatest foolishness, but as we believe, so we act. If we change our group awareness of the meaning of life on this planet, and recognize our interconnectedness, we will create a harmonious life environment.

THE IMPORTANCE OF TALKING TO DUCKS

What does talking to ducks have to do with life as we know it? Perhaps nothing, perhaps everything. It is my opinion that the most significant issue we face today is division and separation; from ourselves, from each other, and from all life.

What does talking to ducks have to do with division and separation? Let's start with why we don't talk to ducks. We don't talk to ducks because we feel superior to ducks and different from ducks. We believe ducks are beneath us and don't matter. They're unimportant unless they're something to look at, hunt, or eat. It is this exaggerated self-importance that has created the division between us and our environment.

Without having a sense of equality with our environment, without a sense of sanctity, interdependence and awe, then one feels separated, different, above it all, and *self-important.* It is only when we feel different, superior, and self-important, that we believe it is necessary or right to destroy people or animals or trees. A person who recognizes his or her interconnectedness with life, recognizes that their very survival depends on their concern and respect for life.

Self-importance, the way I am describing it, originates from a belief that we are different; a belief that we have the right, often the "God-given right", to control, force, change, and ultimately destroy anyone and anything around us that we perceive as different from us. We are so *important* that we pollute the rivers and oceans of the world with petroleum by-products. All so we can drive gasoline engines 70 miles per hour to get to and from our occupations. In doing this, we are polluting the air we breathe that allows trees and plants to grow and in which birds fly.

We can't use solar power or electric power because it might take ten minutes longer to get where we're going, and because we wouldn't reap the same profits from solar and wind power that we do from stripping the earth of its natural resources. These noisy, dangerous machines are destroying the very eco-system on which we depend. We are so *important*, that if other people control natural resources that we believe are necessary for us, we go to that place, subjugate the people there, and strip the land on which they live.

As I am writing, I have two or three ducks here pecking at me, talking to me, jabbering away, because these ducks don't think I'm so important, and because of that, they're willing to be part of what I'm doing. And, when I am able to *not* feel so important, I can stop what I'm doing and spend time getting to know their life, becoming aware of their experience, listening to their way of talking to each other, appreciating their right, just like mine, to be here.

We have separated ourselves too much from the world around us. We have created machines, big ugly looking things, mainly used to manipulate, control, and destroy the environment. We have created ideas, cultures, and societies based on the assumption that we are right and everybody else is wrong. We have created religions whose followers believe that if they don't believe and act like their God demands, they will be punished eternally. *For what?* Just for having different ideas, different thoughts, and different feelings from someone else!

Most of all, we have created enough weapons to destroy this planet over and over again. All designed for one reason or another, to kill our own kind. In the natural world it is very rare that a species kills one of it's own kind. It may happen by accident, sometimes in fits of rage, or in desperate situations. *It's extremely rare.* We have utilized our tool-making capacity to create a technology designed to kill each other and ourselves. We are the great destroyers on this planet. We destroy the sky, the water, the land, all the animals on it, and even ourselves. This *cannot* continue.

I am suggesting a new core belief for our society. The *old* belief, that we are so self-important that we can do anything we want, is not working. The new core belief I am suggesting is: We are neither *more* important nor *less* important than the world around us. We are simply a part of the world around us, much like a piece in a jigsaw puzzle. All the pieces need to be there for the picture to be created, to be seen, to exist, and to endure. We cannot continue to kill off all the various pieces we find unimportant or not useful and expect the picture to remain. Life is what connects us. Life is multi-dimensional, life is small and life is grand, life is long and life is short, life has emotions, life has intelligence, life has organizing principles; some of them individual, some of them collective. Watch a flock of birds quickly flying through the air, all at once they immediately change directions. Individually, they know not where they're going. Collectively, they have organizing principles that precisely directs them to where they need to be at that time.

Life *will* survive. In order for *us* to survive, we once again need to respect the collectiveness of life, the inner commonality, the beauty of relationship. Not only with each other, but with *All That Is.* Time does not end, but we certainly can. We need to learn how to treat ourselves, and our earth-friends, with a loving technology, a loving respect, and an awareness that their survival is our survival.

I am not against technology. I am against technology run rampant with self-importance. I am against a technology that feels too grand or too foolish to talk to ducks. I am against a technology that destroys, with little respect or concern for the effects of that destruction. There are other ways to proceed. We can study life without destroying life. We can experiment without making the experimentee the subject of our objectivity. We can learn to have a technology that immerses itself in life, that uses not only the intellect, but uses intuition, senses, and emotion. There are other kinds of knowledge. Knowledge that grows from wisdom. Wisdom that recognizes the interdependence of all life. The ducks look at me as if to say, "Well, are you just going to keep writing or are you going to get us something to eat?" And it seems to me, that all things being equal, at this moment, getting them something to eat is at least as important as continuing this paragraph. (Quack, quack, quack.)

"Come on guys, time to eat, come here, come here."

"Come on, you too, come on baby, here we go, a little more for you?"

"Okay, that's all for now. Yup, that's all for now, that's all, yeah...."

(Quack, quack, quack)

13

FREEDOM

Footsteps left to let you know
Someone before you has been down this road.
A path of dreams a way to there
The palace that's before you is made of only air.
A journey through one's mind
A place that has no time
The sighting of dimension, some colored misconception,
are all that here you'll find.
So come with me this way where here it is always day,
and listen to the words that I've begun to say.
Let's begin on this walk where with the gods we'll talk
and travel through dimensions where learning is not taught.

What is freedom? And, is it desirable? Or obtainable? Perhaps it is better to first consider what it means to be unfree or trapped. By definition, not being free implies restraint, encumbrance, or blockage.

The most obvious type of not being free is physical incarceration, actually blocking the motion of the physical body in space. This can be from either imprisonment or a disability that prohibits freedom of movement. While this is the most obvious way of being trapped or unfree, it is the least common. Much more common and profound is to be trapped psychologically.

Blocking freedom of motion only restricts the body. Blocking freedom of thought and emotion restricts the Self, the whole person, leaving the person-ality unable to express itself. It is as if the "true" person, the person-ality, that which makes a person person-able, has been restrained and restricted—only able to feel and act within the narrow confines of their own prison of beliefs. This prison goes wherever the person goes. *No one else* has the key to the cell. We must look inside ourselves to find the key that can free us!

To examine how we are trapped we must carefully examine the nature of obsessive/compulsive behavior. Obsessive/compulsive behavior is behavior that we cannot get out of our mind and we feel compelled to do. We believe we have *no* choice and therefore no *freedom* of choice. Our *need* to act and behave in certain ways defines our choices and eliminates our freedom. Freedom means the ability to choose our actions. Obsessive/compulsive behaviors are not *freely* made but driven by *need* rather than choice.

What creates this *need* to behave in certain ways? We get trapped into obsessive/compulsive behaviors by limited beliefs. An example of this is the belief that we are not good enough the way we are. We believe that in order to be loved and accepted we must be different. We believe that we are broken, lacking, and insufficient. The true challenge is to accept oneself, honestly and fully, even when others do not. By doing so one loses the attachment of needing other's approval, thereby losing the obsessive/compulsive behaviors designed to impress others. This condition leads to freedom of choice, or non-attachment, or "enlightenment."

There are no *better* people. Self-worth or universal worth is not predicated on performance or appearance; it is freely and naturally given. Attachment to the belief or idea in *better* creates *not good enough* and the life long attempt to "fix" oneself. There are better tennis players, better writers, and better carpenters but there *are no better people*. One two-year-old is not *better* than another but they are trained, influenced, and hypnotized into believing that they are different, and in order to be *good enough* for love, approval, and acceptance they must be *better* than others through performances, appearance, emotions, or intelligence. This leads to an early felt *lack* in the emerging identity of the child. A lack or deficit that in fact does not exist but is created by the erroneous and limiting beliefs and demands of others, often parental and other authority figures.

Now believing that there is something wrong or some deficiency that makes them unworthy of love and acceptance, the young child appropriately, but erroneously, identifies their core identity or self-worth with these imagined or real *differences* in appearance, emotions, intelligence, or performance. They see these differences as wrong or bad. They believe they must be "fixed" at all costs if they are to ever have a life of love and acceptance.

Now begins a life-long tragic and unnecessary struggle to "fix" what was never "broken", leading to continued perceptions of inadequacy. This creates destructive, spiraling behavior as our "solutions" to these *imagined* problems fuel more life difficulties, which continually reinforce our original beliefs.

By clearly "seeing" the erroneous nature of our perceived sense of inadequacy and insufficiency, we are able to comprehend that if we weren't "broken" *then* we must not be "broken" *now*. We come to the realization that we have been attempting to "fix" something all these years that did not need fixing. All our "solutions" to these unwanted feelings of "badness" and inadequacy were unnecessary. And as the "solutions" were often in the form of obsessive/compulsive behaviors, seeing the futility and nonsensical nature of those behaviors *frees* us to live a life of *our* choosing. Rather than obsessively attempting to be different or better, or obsessively attempting to avoid feelings of inadequacy, we see the false nature of these core beliefs. This allows for the self-acceptance, self-love, and freedom that we have been seeking on this journey.

To have freedom, pleasure, and quality in our life, it is first necessary to explore the inner world of our beliefs. When we find beliefs that are serving us well, those are beliefs that we can consciously promote and reinforce in our daily life. In areas where we are successful, we know that we have core beliefs that are promoting that success. We can then agree with and reinforce these beliefs. In areas where we feel unsuccessful, we know that there are core beliefs that are holding us back, stopping our sense of freedom and joy, and limiting our pleasure. It is necessary to examine these core beliefs, expose them to conscious awareness, and set about a specific program to change these beliefs to ones that are life-giving, rather than life-restricting.

Living in reality, a falsely used word in our society.
To live life in a real matter we must first understand
the means of fantasy.
Combine the two together and enjoy a Fantastic Reality.

AXIOMS OF BELIEF THERAPY

Axiom I   I was born perfect. I was born natural, my
behaviors, feelings, thoughts, and body were
all born *good*. There is *no* original sin!

Axiom II   My dysfunctional behaviors, ideas, self-
judgment, and artificial guilt are a direct
result of limiting beliefs that I have *learned*.
As such, they are wholly and completely
changeable at *all* and *any* time in my life,
throughout my life.

Axiom III   I can trust my feelings. No feeling can hurt
me or another. Feelings are only "paper drag-
ons." They are meant to be trusted and
accepted. It is the *behaviors* that we do to rid
ourselves of feelings that often create our
problems.

Axiom IV   By *fully* accepting ourselves in the present
and recognizing we need not fix what was
never broken, we free ourselves *now* from
limiting ideas and beliefs of the past. This is
the magical approach to life. It is real, truth-
ful, and permanent.

Axiom V   *All* other methods of growth are simply, "trying to fix what was never broken." They can
be useful, time consuming, frustrating, or
perhaps, necessary fillers to bring us to the
jumping off point of **Axiom IV,** but they are
not **Axiom IV.**

Axiom VI   When **Axiom IV** is fully comprehended this
releases the body from unnecessary strain,
stress, and dis-ease allowing natural physical health and harmony and natural well-
being. Acceptance of the self creates and
allows acceptance of the body, leading to
physical, spiritual, and emotional harmony.

131

Axiom VII   Physical, spiritual, and emotional harmony allows and promotes choices and freedom. It is not a static ending but rather a fluid beginning.

Axiom VIII   By believing the **Axioms of Belief Therapy** for myself I recognize that they are equally true for all life, allowing me to live in harmony with others and my environment.

References

Benson, H. *Timeless Healing, The Power and Biology of Belief.* New York: Scribner, 1996.

Simonton, O. C., Matthews-Simonton, S., & Creighton, J.L. *Getting Well Again.* New York: Bantam Books, 1978.

Rotter, J.B. *Social Learning and Clinical Psychology.* Inglewood Cliffs, N.J.: Prentice Hall, 1954.

Clason, G.S. *The Richest Man in Babylon.* New York: Penguin, 1926.

Everyday Life Seminars

If you found yourself feeling hopeful, balanced,
and uplifted after reading
Belief Therapy
"A Guide to Enhancing Everyday Life"
Come spend the day with
Dr. DeGoede & Danaë Drews
at our next Everyday Life Seminar

Topics Covered:

Relationships
Parenting
Addictions
Health
Abuse & Trauma
Violence in America
Religion & Spirituality

The Self
Death & Dying
Personal Finances
Freedom
Codependency
Environment

"To have freedom, pleasure and quality in
our life, it is first necessary to explore the inner
world of our beliefs."

Call Today! (800) 215-4337

Ask for this book at your local bookstore or use this page to order.

Give a gift of freedom & pleasure. *Belief Therapy "A Guide to Enhancing Everyday Life"*

☎ **Telephone Orders:** (800) 215-4337
✉ **Postal Orders:** E.D.L. Productions
P.O. Box 786
Lake Elsinore, CA 92531-0786

❐ Please send ____ copies of *Belief Therapy, "A Guide to Enhancing Everyday Life."*

❐ Please send free information regarding Everyday Life Seminars.

❐ Please send free information regarding other E.D.L. Books/Products.

Company Name:_____

Name:_____

Address: _____

City: _____ State:____ Zip:_____

Telephone: (____) _____

Cost: $12.95 per book. Discounts offered if ordering in quantity.

Sales Tax: Please add 7.75% for books shipped to California addresses.

Shipping: $3.50 for the first book and $2.00 for each additional book.

Payment: Please make check or money order payable to: *E.D.L. Productions*

If paying by MASTERCARD or VISA, please include:

Card Number:_____

Name On Card:_____

Exp. Date: _____ / _____

We look forward to your order!!

Ask for this book at your local bookstore or use this page to order.

Give a gift of freedom & pleasure. ***Belief Therapy "A Guide to Enhancing Everyday Life"***

☎ **Telephone Orders:**   (800) 215-4337
✉ **Postal Orders:**   E.D.L. Productions
                P.O. Box 786
                Lake Elsinore, CA 92531-0786

❐ Please send _____ copies of *Belief Therapy, "A Guide to Enhancing Everyday Life."*

❐ Please send free information regarding Everyday Life Seminars.

❐ Please send free information regarding other E.D.L. Books/Products.

Company Name:_____

Name:_____

Address: _____

City: _____ State:_____ Zip:_____

Telephone: (_____) _____

Cost: $12.95 per book. Discounts offered if ordering in quantity.

Sales Tax: Please add 7.75% for books shipped to California addresses.

Shipping: $3.50 for the first book and $2.00 for each additional book.

Payment: Please make check or money order payable to: *E.D.L. Productions*

If paying by MASTERCARD or VISA, please include:

Card Number:_____

Name On Card:_____

Exp. Date: _____ / _____

We look forward to your order!!

Notes

Notes